SHORT CUTS

INTRODUCTIONS TO FILM STUDIES

WOMEN'S CINEMA

THE CONTESTED SCREEN

ALISON BUTLER

WALLFLOWER

LONDON and NEW YORK

A Wallflower Paperback

First published in Great Britain in 2002 by Wallflower Press, reprinted 2005
6a Middleton Place, Langham Street, London, W1W 7TE
www.wallflowerpress.co.uk

A catalogue record for this book is available from the British Library

ISBN 1 903364 27 2

Book Design by Rob Bowden Design

Printed in Great Britain by Antony Rowe Ltd, Chippenham, Wiltshire

CONTENTS

LIST OF ILLUSTRATIONS

ACKNOWLEDGEMENTS

I have taught women's cinema in several forms over the past decade, and would like to thank the students at the University of Bristol and the University of Reading who took my courses for making them enjoyable and informative. I am grateful to members of the University of Reading for supporting my work on this book in a number of ways, through the Research Endowment Trust Fund, and through the many kinds of assistance I have received from colleagues in the Department of Film and Drama.

This book was conceived at the same time as a baby, and completed soon after his birth; it would not have been finished at all without the considerable support and forbearance of my family, John, Djuna and Jackson Mount, for which I thank them.

This book is dedicated to Djuna.

INTRODUCTION: FROM COUNTER-CINEMA TO MINOR CINEMA

> I see my own work as a kind of 'minor literature' – in the sense that Deleuze and Guattari talk about this, 'like a dog digging a hole, like a rat digging its burrow', working through the language that is given to us, in this case, that of dominant cinema and the historical avant-garde. They speak about being nomads, immigrants, Gypsies in relation to one's own language. (Leslie Thornton in Jayamanne *et al.* 1992: 250)

Women's cinema is a notoriously difficult concept to define. It suggests, without clarity, films that might be made by, addressed to, or concerned with women, or all three. It is neither a genre nor a movement in film history, it has no single lineage of its own, no national boundaries, no filmic or aesthetic specificity, but traverses and negotiates cinematic and cultural traditions and critical and political debates. It could potentially – or might not – embrace practitioners as diverse as Hollywood producer Dawn Steel on the one hand, and queer-cinema doyenne Christine Vachon on the other, and directors ranging from Kathryn Bigelow, famous for her spectacular genre pictures, to Joyce Wieland, whose best-known movie starred gerbils. A female film-maker's body of work might intersect with women's cinema on occasion, but not consistently, as in the case of Maggie Greenwald, director of a hard-boiled pulp fiction, *The Kill-Off* (1989), and the cross-dressed feminist western *The Ballad of*

Little Jo (1993). Alternatively, a film-maker may contribute significantly to women's cinema and to another cinema at the same time, as Julie Dash has done consistently, and particularly with *Daughters of the Dust* (1991), a landmark within both women's cinema and African-American cinema. Some of the most distinguished practitioners of women's cinema have deliberately distanced themselves from the notion, for professional and/or political reasons, to avoid marginalisation or ideological controversy (as in the case of Larissa Shepitko, who, like many in Eastern Europe, considered the concept of women's cultural production inegalitarian; Chantal Akerman, who, despite her cult following among feminists, prefers to be seen as an auteur like any other, or the many women directors in contemporary Iranian cinema whose professional existence depends on avoiding ideological confrontation). Their work, nevertheless, continues to be pulled into spaces of exhibition, criticism and debate defined in terms of gender, such as women's festivals, conferences, courses and publications like this one.

'Women's cinema' is a complex critical, theoretical and institutional construction, brought into existence by audiences, film-makers, journalists, curators and academics and maintained only by their continuing interest: a hybrid concept, arising from a number of overlapping practices and discourses, and subject to a baffling variety of definitions. It is beyond the scope of this book to map the extensive history of women's film-making and feminist criticism in its entirety. Instead, the chapters which follow offer critical perspectives on women's practices within some of the major cinema traditions and at the same time indicate some of the most significant debates around the concept of women's cinema in anglophone film theory. In this introductory chapter, I will outline some of the founding debates of the 1970s and indicate their legacy for women's cinema and feminist criticism.

Feminist film theory and women's cinema

Women have been involved in film-making since the invention of the cinema, but the idea of a women's cinema as such is much more recent, dating from the late 1960s and early 1970s, when the ferment of the women's movement pervaded every aspect of cultural and social life, including film culture. Film festivals and film journals began the work of recovering the history of women's creativity in cinema; women film-makers began, in groups and singly, to produce avowedly feminist films; and in the new field of Film Studies feminism quickly made its mark. By the end of the 1970s, however, the tendency to schism that has accompanied so much feminist activity was also evident in feminist film culture which, in the words of Teresa de Lauretis, had become split between

> two types of film work that seemed to be at odds with each other: one called for immediate documentation for purposes of political activism, consciousness-raising, self-expression, or the search for 'positive images' of woman; the other insisted on rigorous, formal work on the medium – or, better, the cinematic apparatus, understood as a social technology – in order to analyze and disengage the ideological codes embedded in representation. (de Lauretis 1987b: 128)

The influence of this division has been formative, insofar as the need for these two tendencies to rejoin has shaped theoretical and critical debate around women's cinema ever since, even when it has not been recognised.

A number of factors contributed to feminist film theory's move away from its grassroots, including the decline of the women's movement, the arrival in the UK and the US of continental European theories of ideology, semiotics and psychoanalysis which had developed in the wake of structural linguistics, and the rapid development of a number of new disciplines, including Film Studies and Women's Studies. In this context, feminist film theory flourished. Women's film-making, on the other hand, did not develop at the same rate or, generally, in the same direction. The gradual increase in the still small numbers of women working in film stems from the broader impact of feminist politics and other social changes rather than from the impact of feminist film theory, and when films embody feminist thinking it is usually drawn from fields other than film theory (there are notable exceptions, including the films of Kathryn Bigelow and Sally Potter). In the absence of a practice to call its own, early feminist film theory was driven by debates within the emergent field of Film Studies, and conceptualised the women's cinema of the future in response to a set of problematics arising from the conjuncture of film theory and Hollywood cinema.

Central among these problematics were the relations of the look, the ideological implications of narrative forms, and the effects of spectator-positioning on subject construction. The ground-breaking work of Laura Mulvey and Claire Johnston, among others, displaced questions about women's positive or negative, realistic or distorted representation, in order to articulate challenging questions about the nature and ideological effects of the medium. Feminist film theory was founded on the proposition, also central to John Berger's *Ways of Seeing* (1972), that looking and being looked at are charged with sexual and social power relations:

> *Men act* and *women appear.* Men look at women. Women watch themselves being looked at. This determines not only most rela-tions between men and women, but also the relation of women to themselves. The surveyor of woman in herself is male: the surveyed female. Thus she turns herself into an object – and most particu-larly an object of vision – a sight. (Berger 1972: 47)

The male gaze was described in the vocabulary of psychoanalytic theorist Jacques Lacan: scopophilia, voyeurism, fetishism and narcissism were the modalities of a controlling, punishing, self-regarding look which functioned to assuage the male subject's castration anxiety at the expense of the feminine (see Kaplan 1983). Following Freud, the organisation of sexual difference in the cinema was understood in terms of the binary equation of activity with mascu-linity and passivity with femininity. Narrative systems were analysed in the light of structuralist work on functions and Roland Barthes' notion of narrative codes, from which it was concluded that in linear narrative 'Woman' operates conventionally to signify an enigma, obstacle or prize for a male protagonist, and, by implication, a male or masculinised spectator. From ideological theories of the cinematic apparatus, feminists adopted the idea that spectatorship functions analogously to subject formation, and that mainstream cinema's address to its spectators functions to preserve the illusion of unified subjectivity upon which bourgeois ideology depends. In this account, 'Woman' is at once an empty sign and a completely co-opted icon, as Claire Johnston argues: 'Woman represents not herself, but by a process of displacement, the male phallus. It is probably true to say that despite the enormous emphasis placed on woman as spectacle in the cinema, woman as woman is largely absent' (1973b: 25–6).

The feminist theorists of the 1970s were correct in noting the scarcity of female points of view in studio period Hollywood films, Freudian psychoanalysis and post-structural theory, but erroneous in treating these absences as evidence of the absolute alterity of the feminine as such, rather than inscriptions of the gendered subjectivities of their creators. The ambitions of feminism in film were narrowed to the exercise of a female gaze, female desire, and female narrative agency; objectives which might have seemed quite achievable if they had not been pinned to the matrix of post-structural psychoanalytic theory. The questionable analogies between cinematic identification, ideological interpellation and subject formation which gained acceptance in feminist film studies brought unrealistic expectations of cultural revolution to bear on cinematic innovation. For feminist film-making, then, the argument that sexism was embedded in film at the level of form, and even designed into the cinematic apparatus, had profound implications, summed up by B. Ruby Rich:

> According to Mulvey, the woman is not visible in the audience which is perceived as male; according to Johnston, the woman is not visible on the screen. She is merely a surrogate for the phallus, a signifier for something else, etc. As a woman going into the movie theater, you are faced with a context that is coded wholly for your invisibility, and yet, obviously, you are sitting there and bringing along a certain coding from outside the theater. (Rich *et al.* 1978: 87)

Rich's comments set out the agenda which structured debate in feminist film studies and informed the aesthetics of feminist counter-cinema for twenty years.

Mulvey: counter-cinema as negative aesthetics

The account of feminist film theory offered above is a distillation from a number of texts, indicating a core of ideas which feminist theorists engaged with, although very few, if any, held to all of them dogmatically. Likewise, though many theorists rallied to the cause of a feminist counter-cinema, their conceptions of what this would involve varied considerably. Nowhere is this more true than in the early writings of its two major theorists, Laura Mulvey and Claire Johnston. In 'Visual Pleasure and Narrative Cinema', Mulvey concludes her devastating polemic against mainstream narrative film by advocating the creation of 'a new language of desire' to 'free the look of the camera into its materiality in time and space and the look of the audience into dialectics, passionate detachment' (1975: 8). Women, she argues, should view the decline of traditional film form (which, in 1975, appeared a real possibility) with nothing more than 'sentimental regret' (18).

In 'Film, Feminism and the Avant-Garde', Mulvey addresses the question of feminist aesthetics more directly, beginning with the problem of where women's cinematic aesthetics should come from, in the absence of a discernible female tradition. She argues against attempting to infer a tradition from the fragmentary history of women's cultural work under patriarchy, on the grounds that 'the new grows only out of the work of confrontation' (1979: 4). Dismissing the possibilities for feminist work within the mainstream on the one hand, and the prospect of the emergence of a feminist aesthetic *de novo* on the other, Mulvey envisages women's cinema as counter-cinema in the oppositional tradition of political modernism. She regards avant-garde cinema, with its history of schism and innovation, as a model for feminist film and a store-house of strategies of defamiliarisation, rupture and reflexivity, including, crucially, Bertholt Brecht's alienation effects and Jean-Luc Godard's pedagogic formalism:

> An important aspect of avant-garde aesthetics is negation: a work
> is formed, or driven to adopt a particular position, by the very code
> itself of the dominant tradition that is being opposed. These works

have then to be read, achieve meaning, in the reflected light of the aesthetics they negate. One aspect of the problems implicit in the formulation of a new aesthetic is thus circumvented. (9)

Mulvey's avant-gardism places her in the tradition of feminist modernism from Virginia Woolf to Julia Kristeva. In an essay on melodrama, Mulvey comments on the betrayal of cinema's modernity, specifically by D. W. Griffith, who brought the spectacle and sentiment of late Victorian theatre into silent cinema, and with them 'a conscious political stance that was already conservative and nostalgic': 'There seems, in Griffith's work, to be a desperate refusal to acknowledge the modernity of the cinema, the contemporary world and its aesthetics and, particularly, a new and changing concept of womanhood' (1986: 86). Writing in 1926, Virginia Woolf is similarly critical of the predominance of melodrama and stereotype in silent film, and imagines an alternative future for the medium as 'something abstract, something which moves with controlled and conscious art [in which] we should be able to see thought in its wildness, in its beauty, in its oddity' (1996: 36). However, while Woolf represents the positive projects of feminism and modernism, seeking new forms for modern consciousness, Mulvey's 1970s stance is closer to the negation advocated by Julia Kristeva, writing almost fifty years later, in the context of second-wave feminism:

A feminist practice can only be negative, at odds with what already exists so that we may say 'that's not it' and 'that's still not it'. In 'woman' I see something that cannot be represented, something that is not said, something beyond nomenclatures and ideologies (1981: 137)

Within feminist film theory, this argument has been immensely influential in stating the negation of visual and narrative pleasure at the heart of feminist aesthetics (for more on this debate see Kuhn 1982; Kaplan 1983) and contributing to the formation of a feminist canon, dominated by cinematic counterparts of the theory in the work of formalist film-makers such as Chantal Akerman, Marguerite Duras, Bette Gordon, Sally Potter, Yvonne Rainer and Helke Sander.

At the same time, this tendency has been questioned and opposed by critics who have disputed its political effectiveness and its artistic inclusiveness. Christine Gledhill notes that negative aesthetics risk indefinitely postponing the production of meaning which is essential to political art, 'dissolving the subject in an endless play of radical difference' (1994: 117). Anneke Smelik complains of the 'largely unjustified acclaim of experimental women's cinema among the elected few who get to see it' (1998: 12) and points out the paradox of requiring female spectators to renounce visual pleasures already denied to them. Mulvey concedes that negation was a strategy of its time, never intended as an end in itself, but rather designed to facilitate a decisive break: 'Counter-aesthetics, too, can harden into a system of dualistic opposition' (1987: 8).

In the 1970s, it made sense to conceive counter-cinema solely in terms of opposition to an enfeebled mainstream industry, but by the mid-1980s, the revival of Hollywood and the rise of new forms of political and cultural conservatism had created a need for other models. Economic and cultural forces overtook the argument for an aesthetic of negation. In retrospect, it seems fair to say that although women have created many brilliant works within the avant-garde since the 1970s, their achievements lie in their re-inflections of *its* practices rather than their effective opposition to the mainstream. At the same time, women have gradually made small inroads into feature film production, and have begun to change mainstream cinema from within. Intimations of a critical aesthetic which works *within* mainstream forms can be found in Mulvey's writing on the melodramas of Douglas Sirk, but a more extended exploration of such possibilities exists in the writing of Claire Johnston, which draws on the tradition of progressive cinephilia's reevaluation of the entertainment film in order to envisage a non-formalist women's cinema.

Johnston: counter-cinema as discursive struggle

'Women's Cinema as Counter-Cinema' has become a canonical text in Film Studies, but when it was published in 1973, it flew in the face of most of the thinking about cinema that had emerged from the women's movement. In her introduction to *Notes on Women's Cinema*, the pamphlet in which her best-known essay first appeared, Claire Johnston comes out against the stance of early 1970s feminist film criticism which 'takes as its starting point the manipulation of women as sexual objects by the media' (1973a: 3). This view, she claims, articulates a puritanical distrust of entertainment and spectacle in general and overlooks the particularity of the cinema. It comes from a long tradition of bourgeois criticism:

> The analysis of Hollywood as a 'dream machine' producing a monolithic product is in fact a very conventional view which has been held by reactionary film critics for decades. It expresses a distaste for 'the masses', and an elitism which sees in the growth of the great popular art of the twentieth century the danger of the 'erosion' of 'artistic values'. (3)

When Johnston wrote this, she was allying herself to a different critical tradition, initiated by the reevaluation of American cinema undertaken by *Cahiers du cinéma*. Like the post-1968 critics of the influential French journal, she argues for Marxist ideological analysis, but also for entertainment and fantasy. Johnston relates her non-formalist commitment to the entertainment film to the question of pleasure: political cinema aims to produce and disseminate knowledge, but cannot accomplish this without also generating pleasure. Women's cinema, she argues, should learn from the successes of Hollywood: 'In order to counter our objectification in the cinema, our collective fantasies must be released: women's cinema must embody the working through of desire: such an objective demands the use of the entertainment film' (1973b: 31).

While acknowledging the disproportionate institutional and economic power of Hollywood, Johnston argues that this does not necessarily deprive its products of internal complexity and heterogeneity. Following Comolli and Narboni's influential *Cahiers du cinéma* editorial (1971), she argues that studio films may function counter-hegemonically if they contain enough ideological contradictions. Comolli and Narboni offer a political taxonomy of films, ranging from those which consistently reinforce traditional ideology, to those which are revolutionary in both content and form. Hollywood films appear in the former category, but also in a special category of films in which ideology fails to cohere, producing contradiction in the text. Johnston writes:

> This internal criticism facilitates a process of de-naturalisation; behind the film's apparent coherence there exists an 'internal tension' so that the ideology no longer has an independent existence but is 'presented' by the film. The pressure of this tension cracks open the surface of the film; instead of its ideology being simply assumed and therefore virtually invisible, it is revealed and made explicit. (1975: 3)

Overturning received feminist wisdom, Johnston proposes that Hollywood's reliance on stereotypes renders it particularly liable to subversion: 'myth uses icons, but the icon is its weakest point' (1973b: 25). The less realistic the icon the better, as verisimilitude naturalises iconography, whereas obvious stereotypicality is always in some sense reflexive: it points to textuality, and to the place of the text in a cultural tradition. Johnston sees this process at work in the films of Dorothy Arzner, Nelly Kaplan and others:

> In fact, because iconography offers in some ways a greater resistance to the realist characterisations [of male personae], the mythic qualities of certain stereotypes become far more easily detachable and can be used as a short-hand for referring to an ideological tradition in order to provide a critique of it. It is possible to disengage the icons from the myth and thus bring about reverberations within the sexist ideology in which the film is made. (1975: 3)

In 'Dorothy Arzner: Critical Strategies', Johnston describes the dislocation of patriarchal discourse within Arzner's films in terms of the artistic device of 'ostranenie', or estrangement, as described by Victor Shklovsky. Arzner's textual system, according to Johnston, juxtaposes male and female discourses, and although the narratives are not – and within classical Hollywood conventions cannot be – resolved in favour of female discourse, the woman's point of view displaces and ironises patriarchal ideology:

> In all these cases, the discourse of the woman fails to triumph *over* the male discourse and the patriarchal ideology, but its very survival in the form of irony is in itself a kind of triumph, a victory against being expelled or erased: the continued insistence of the woman's discourse is a triumph over non-existence. (1975: 7)

Arzner is seen as a protofeminist rather than a feminist, but the rewriting process which Johnston describes ('the discourse of the woman is the principal structuring element which rewrites the dominant discourse of the film together with the patriarchal ideology into which it locks' (8)) is at the heart of her thinking about feminist counter-cinema. The importance of Arzner, she states, is that 'her films pose the problem for all of us: is it possible to sweep aside the existing forms of discourse in order to found a new language?' (8). Unlike Mulvey, Johnston argues for the elaboration of feminist discourse within the interstices of conventional forms. In this, she anticipates the postmodern preoccupation with appropriation, citation and rewriting ('These women do not sweep aside the existing order and found a new, female, order of language. Rather, they assert their own discourse in the face of the male one, by breaking it up, subverting it and, in a sense, rewriting it' (4)). Her definition of women's cinema is based on the same methodological presupposition as Anne Freadman's definition of women's writing:

> That any text is a rewriting of the field or fields of its own emergence, that to write, to read, or to speak is first of all to turn other texts into discursive material, displacing the enunciative position from which those materials have been propounded. I mean that 'use' can always do something a little different from merely repeating 'usage'. In an attempt to do something towards specifying 'women's writing', I shall suppose that it is in the business of transforming discursive material that, in its untransformed state leaves a woman no place from which to speak, or nothing to say. (cited in Morris 1988: 3)

Taking issue with the premise that classical Hollywood cinema locks the spectator into a fixed position which encourages fetishistic reading, Johnston argues that a film is composed of a 'specific hierarchy of interrelated discourses' (1975: 3), which, in the case of the progressive classical text, may contradict and question each other. In the interplay between these discourses, through contestation and subversion, the male point of view may be displaced by the female. In Ida Lupino's films she finds 'reverberations within the narrative, produced by the convergence of two irreconcilable strands – Hollywood myths of woman v the female perspective – [which] cause a series of distortions within the very structure of the narrative' (1973b: 30). In Nelly Kaplan's films, Johnston regards generic intertextuality – references to Hollywood genres and cartoon imagery within an art film – as the principal tactic of a feminist surrealism.

In Johnston's work until the late 1970s these enabling ideas co-exist (in contradiction) with a Lacanian feminist model of spectatorship and subjectivity. By the end of the decade she had concluded that 'work on text/subject relations which aims to transform the relationship between text and viewer cannot be seen as a goal in itself' (1980: 29). Instead, she turned to the 'conjunctural analysis' of cinema as a social practice, embedded within a social and cultural formation, and in her last published essay on women's cinema,[1] '*Maeve*', advocates:

> A move away from the notion of 'text' and 'spectator' conceptualised in abstract and a-historical terms and towards a more interventionist conception of textual practice seen within specific historical conjunctures, where formalist criteria for assessing whether a film is 'progressive' or 'reactionary' are secondarised. (1981: 92)

Her reading of *Maeve* (Pat Murphy, Ireland/UK, 1981) traces the film's articulation, through its protagonist, the Northern Irish exile Maeve, of two incompatible discourses: republicanism (with its ties to Catholicism) and feminism. The film uses narrative and identification, but, Johnston argues, works within *and* against their conventional deployment. She proposes that the film is concerned with women's negative relation to language and the Symbolic, but specifies this exclusion in historical

terms: Maeve is outside of republican discourse and patriarchal nationalist culture. Her struggle to enter into this culture is essentially a struggle
to displace the nationalist imaginary, in which women function as passive
objects in a conflict between men or embodiments of a mythic, maternal
Ireland, to construct instead an alternative imaginary for women, in
which they might figure as historical agents. Maeve is not a 'positive
heroine', but she is a point of identification, engaged with the *possibility*
of creating positive images for women. Johnston suggests that the film
uses this identification precisely to address the problem of identity, and
that Murphy, like Arzner, articulates the woman's situation by pitting
discourse against discourse: 'If the dominant discourse works to natu-
ralise ideologies and culture, the feminine discourse works to de-natu-
ralise it, producing a space which must be filled, a problem of identity
and position within the text' (93).

The value of an approach which prioritises discursive structures over
looking relations has been drawn out by Christine Gledhill, in her essay
'Image and Voice', in which she argues that the theory of woman as sign
leads to a dead end as far as cultural struggle is concerned, whereas the
notion of women's discourse allows for contestation and negotiation.
The usefulness of the concept of women's discourse, Gledhill suggests,
derives from the way that it cuts across the division between text and
society, and in doing so, 'draws discourses circulating in society and in
other cultural forms into the fabric of the film' (1994: 118). The notion
of discourse also functions as an antidote to formalism: unlike a formal
strategy, which manifests itself systematically throughout the text in
the same register or registers of expression, a discourse may be distributed across the film discontinuously, through a variety of articulations,
which may be aesthetic, semantic, ideological and social. The concept
of discourse allows theorists and film-makers to sidestep hegemonic
aesthetics without rushing into the hermetic embrace of formalism.

De Lauretis: rethinking women's cinema

Among those theorists for whom Claire Johnston's theory of women's
cinema has functioned as a touchstone, Teresa de Lauretis in particular

has refined and developed the critical tradition which she created. In her work, the concept of women's cinema meets the theoretical challenges and cultural changes of the 1980s and 1990s. From the outset, de Lauretis proposes an approach which is reconstructive rather than deconstructive:

> The present task of women's cinema may not be the destruction of narrative and visual pleasure, but rather the construction of another frame of reference, one in which the measure of desire is no longer just the male subject. For what is at stake is not so much how to 'make visible the invisible' as how to produce the conditions of representability for a different social subject. (1984: 8–9)

As in Johnston's writing, performance and citation figure prominently in de Lauretis's argument that feminist films, readings and writings must enact the contradiction between women as historical subjects and Woman as sign: 'To perform the terms of the production of woman as text, as image, is to resist identification with that image. It is to have stepped through the looking glass' (1984: 36).

In a series of essays written during the 1980s, de Lauretis comes to see narrative as essential to feminist cinema. Agreeing with the premise that narrative is the structure within which positionalities of desire and identification are worked out, de Lauretis points out that the only way to renegotiate these is by working 'with and against' it. In the films of Yvonne Rainer, where a growing feminist awareness is accompanied by an increasing narrativity, she argues that narrative produces not only closure, i.e. the false resolutions of hegemonic ideology, but also *coherence*, i.e. meaning:

> Narrative and narrativity, because of their capacity to inscribe desire and to direct, sustain, or undercut identification (in all the senses of the term), are mechanisms to be deployed strategically and tactically in the effort to construct other forms of coherence, to shift the terms of representation, to produce the conditions of representability of another – and gendered – social subject. (1987a: 109)

By making processes of identification central to feminist aesthetics, de Lauretis moves away from the auteurist focus on the director which characterises Johnston's work, and towards the notion of a 'readerly' text. She develops this line of thought in response to feminist films of the 1980s in which she perceives 'an aesthetic of reception' (1987b: 141), a conscious effort to address the spectator as female, which 'allows the film to draw into its discursive texture something of that "Real" which is the untheorized experience of women' (1987a: 119).

Re-focusing attention towards the spectator of feminist film was one way of coming to terms with the explosion of identity politics in feminism in the 1980s: the spectator is addressed as *a* woman, not as Woman, taking into account the intersections of gender with class, race, age and sexuality, acknowledging differences among women as well as differences between women and men. 'Rethinking Women's Cinema' centres on a reading of Lizzie Borden's *Born in Flames* (1983), a science fiction film depicting a feminist uprising in which women from several classes, cultures and subcultures mobilise successfully by acknowledging, and finding strength in, their differences. De Lauretis regards the foregrounding of black characters (and performers) in a film directed by a white woman as particularly important, not because it supplements a 'lack' in white feminism (although at the time that she wrote this, white feminism's neglect of questions of race was a subject of heated debate), but because it creates more complex identificatory possibilities, addressing the spectator as 'female in gender and multiple or heterogeneous in race and class' (1987b: 144). She quotes Borden on the film's address to its audience:

What I was trying to do (and using humour as a way to try to do it) was to have various positions in which everyone had a place on some level. Every woman – with men it is a whole different question – would have some level of identification with a position in the film ... Basically, none of the positioning of black characters was *against* any of the white viewers but more of an invitation: come and work with us. Instead of telling the viewer that he or she could *not* belong, the viewer was supposed to be a repository for all these different points

of view and all these different styles of rhetoric. Hopefully, one would
be able to identify with one position but be able to evaluate all of the
various positions presented in the film. (140)

De Lauretis's position here should not be mistaken for multiculturalism:
she is not proposing a women's cinema in which spectators identify
with their own likenesses on a one-to-one basis, black women with
black women, white women with white women, and so on. Rather, she
is hypothesising a women's cinema in which the flexibility of cinematic
identification provides the formal means to explore the particularity,
multiplicity and mutability of social identities. In her own words: 'the
concept of heterogeneity in the audience also entails a heterogeneity of,
or in, the individual spectator' (142).

In 'Guerrilla in the Midst' (1990), de Lauretis moves from describing
the mode of address of women's cinema to situating it in a political
context. Again, she argues that women's cinema is concerned with the
representability of women as social subjects, and that this involves
formal strategies of contradiction and contestation (the project to work
with and against narrative, shifting the place of the look, playing with
genre/gender crossing and reversal' (9)). However, where her earlier work
seems to assume the positioning of women's cinema in an uncomplicated
way on the continuum of 'alternative' film which includes independent,
avant-garde and third cinema (or at least allows the reader to do so), here
she defines women's cinema quite differently, in terms of its capacity to
identify and address actual communities, foregrounding marginal or
emergent groups within feminism, and, interestingly, working against its
'imaginary self-coherence':

In sum, what I would call alternative films in women's cinema
are those which engage the current problems, the real issues,
the things actually at stake in feminist communities on a local
scale, and which, although informed by a global perspective, do
not assume or aim at a universal, multinational audience, but
address a particular one in its specific history of struggles and
emergency. (17)

De Lauretis argues for a definition of women's cinema which crosses the boundaries between avant-garde and narrative cinema, independent and mainstream, but which is rigorously exclusive on political grounds. This aspect of de Lauretis's thinking has been carried forward by Anneke Smelik who defines feminist cinema in terms of the centrality it grants to female subjectivity (of authors and spectators), conceived as a position in 'a network of power relations of which sexual difference is a major constitutive factor along with others like race, class, sexual preference, age' (1998: 3). Through 'focalization', she claims, narrative films inscribe women's perspectives and engage with feminist issues and women's experience. Smelik's work completes the cycle of a return to narrative in feminist theory and draws critical attention to the tradition of women's narrative film-making in European cinemas.

As well as responding to the theoretical and formal problematics that were the legacy of the 1970s, de Lauretis's rethinking of women's cinema is a response to the shifts that took place in feminism in the 1980s, when the white, heterosexual presumptions which feminist film theory inherited from its psychoanalytic framework began to attract criticism from many directions (for example Stacey 1987; Gaines 1988; hooks 1992). Up to a point, the debate was additive and corrective, forcing theorists to think in specific and material ways about the aesthetics and politics of women's cinema. De Lauretis argues that 'feminism can exist despite those [racial, cultural, sexual] differences, and, as we are just beginning to understand, cannot exist without them' (1987b: 139). However, the very strength and vitality of the other enterprises which also claimed the allegiance of many women film-makers and writers – queer theory and cinema, third cinema, post-colonial cinema, to name but a few – inevitably blurred the bound- aries of women's cinema as a critical and cinematic field. In the 1990s, as hybridity became the watchword in cultural theory, women's cinema too occurred in hybrid forms, like the African-American woman's film *Daugh- ters of the Dust* or the queer feminist costume drama *Orlando* (1992), nor is the feminist canon fixed in this respect: Dorothy Arzner has been reclaimed as a lesbian director (Mayne 1994) and Chantal Akerman has been discussed under the various guises of Belgian, Jew, francophone, exile and lesbian auteur (Foster 1999).

Intertextuality: Fischer, Mayne, Mellencamp and Modleski

The revisionist tradition founded by Johnston and developed by de Lauretis has been advanced since the late 1980s by a number of books, including Lucy Fischer's *Shot/Countershot* (1989), Judith Mayne's *The Woman at the Keyhole* (1990), Patricia Mellencamp's *A Fine Romance* (1995) and Tania Modleski's *Old Wives' Tales* (1999). All of these books define women's cinema in terms of relations of intertextuality with hegemonic cinema traditions.

Fischer's book is framed as a response to the dilemmas of the feminist art historian: whether to conceptualise women's art as an alternative cultural heritage or to situate it within pre-existent traditions and whether to view the work of women artists as gendered or androgynous creation. Fischer proposes a middle way, based in a historical rather than essentialist conception of female identity and cultural production: 'a unity may be found in women's collective dissension from the mainstream culture – a revolt that arises from historical rather than archetypal exigencies' (1989: 7). She argues that because women's art emerges in a dialogical relationship with patriarchal tradition, it is marked by an unusual degree of intertextuality. Each chapter of her book is thus devoted to reading women's films against conventional films, as virtual – although generally not literal – remakes.

Mayne sees women's cinema as a feminist reinvention of film which reworks conventions of narrative and narration, authorship and spectacle, to create the formal conditions for inscriptions of female desire and points of view. She moves away from the dualism which prevails in much of the feminist writing about film by treating forms and conventions as permeable boundaries between one set of possibilities and another, rather than impenetrable borders.

Mellencamp maps the development of film feminism – by which she means feminist theory, historical research and films – over five stages of development: intellectual, irascible, experimental, empirical and economical. She places texts in relation to the intertext of romance as a Hollywood genre and cultural mode, in order to create an inclusive model of women's cinema which builds a tradition from a plurality of broadly feminist perspectives. Unlike most other theorists of women's cinema, she includes mainstream film-makers like Nora Ephron and Martha Coolidge in a feminist continuum, albeit at its less radical end.

Finally Modleski's book responds to a return to genre which is evident in progressive American cinema and culture, and examines the ways that recent works by women engage with established genres. Although 'genre, with its conventions and the security provided by predictable endings, represents stasis and fixity and thus appears at odds with a project that seeks evidence of psychic and social transformations' (1999: 9–10), the works Modleski studies, in a range of genres from the western to the romance, display quite a high degree of fluidity and mutability. Modleski regards genre as an intertext which mediates between aspects of reality, although she draws no general conclusions about the social significance of the current fashion for genre-crossing. All of these studies combine a pluralistic approach to film styles with attention to the specificity of each. No longer in pursuit of 'a feminist film practice', the authors acknowledge that in contemporary cinema, women produce feminist work in a wide variety of forms and styles.

Women's cinema as minor cinema

The plurality of forms, concerns and constituencies in contemporary women's cinema now exceeds even the most flexible definition of counter-cinema. Women's cinema now seems 'minor' rather than oppositional. The idea of the minor comes from Gilles Deleuze and Felix Guattari's concept of minor literature, elaborated in *Kafka: Toward a Minor Literature*.[2] A minor literature is not like a literary genre or period, nor is classification as minor an artistic evaluation – Franz Kafka, after all, is a canonical author, as are other writers and artists whom Deleuze and Guattari place in this category, including James Joyce, Samuel Beckett and Jean-Luc Godard. A minor literature is the literature of a minority or marginalised group, written, not in a minor language, but in a major one, just as Kafka, a Czech Jew, wrote in German. Whilst warning against 'shaky analogies' and romantic celebration of marginality, Meaghan Morris has pointed out the congruence of Claire Johnston's work on women's cinema with Deleuze and Guattari's question: 'How many people today live in a language that is not their own? Or no longer, or not yet, even know their own and know poorly the major language that they are forced to use?' (Deleuze & Guattari 1986: 19):

> While it refers to the experience of immigrants and colonised people, this question is echoed obliquely in the concerns of early feminist criticism and Johnston's work on 'women's films made *within the system*' of Hollywood's social and cinematic codes. A minor literature is not 'marginal', it is what a minority constructs *in a major language*, and so it is a model of action from a colonised position *within* a given society. In this it differs from theories that propose, like Laura Mulvey's early work in film, to found an alternative system. (Morris 1998: xvii)

The analogy upon which the adoption of this concept depends is by no means new in feminist film criticism. As B. Ruby Rich writes: 'our experience is like that of the exile, whom Brecht once singled out as the ultimate dialectician for that daily working out of cultural oppositions in a single body' (1998: 73). Moreover, the three defining features of a minor literature as listed by Deleuze and Guattari are instantly recognisable as characteristics shared by women's cinema (and, indeed, most feminist activity): displacement, dispossession, or, as they term it, deterritorialisation; a sense of everything as political; and a tendency for everything to take on a collective value. In major literatures, the social milieu may serve as 'mere environment or a background' (Deleuze & Guattari 1986: 17) for the individual concerns of the narrative, but in a minor literature, every individual issue matters: 'its cramped space forces each individual intrigue to connect immediately to politics. The individual concern thus becomes all the more necessary, indispensable, magnified, because a whole other story is vibrating within it' (17). Because a minor literature emerges from a deterritorialised group, its function is to conjure up collectivity, even in the absence of an active community:

> Literature finds itself positively charged with the role and function of collective, and even revolutionary, enunciation. It is literature

that produces an active solidarity in spite of skepticism; and if the writer is in the margins or completely outside his or her fragile community, this situation allows the writer all the more possibility to express another possible community and to forge the means for another consciousness and another sensibility. (17)

This notion of a minor literature as involved in the *projection* of a community rather than its *expression* is especially useful to the argument that the existence of a women's cinema need not be premised on an essentialist understanding of the category 'women'. The communities imagined by women's cinema are as many and varied as the films it comprises, and each is involved in its own historical moment. Thinking of (some) women's cultural production as 'minor' (in some ways) does not depend on a belief in women's absolute alienation from language and culture, unlike the 'women's writing' theorised by Kristeva and others, but posits instead a mediated and contestatory relationship:

Even when the author is in the position of a minority and disempowered by the phallocentric nature of the apparatus, the metalinguistic status of the latter demands that all texts be produced within its terms: the codes and language of the Holly-wood model become ineluctable vehicles. The necessity of writing in a dominant language from which one is also excluded does not indicate mere subjugation however, but a significant degree of infil-tration, and thus potency. (Islam 1995: 99)

However, this is not to limit the minor to the strategic infiltration of the mainstream: many of the examples of minor practices offered by Deleuze and Guattari are famously experimental. Indeed, one of the strengths of the concept is its ability to connect radical aesthetics with popular expe-rience: 'What is unusual about *Kafka* is that in place of an avant-garde negation of art's status in bourgeois society, Deleuze and Guattari offer an *affirmative* project based on a mass historical experience' (Morris 1998: xvii). To call women's cinema a minor cinema, then, is to free it from the binarisms (popular/elitist, avant-garde/mainstream, positive/

negative) which result from imagining it as a parallel or oppositional cinema.

The assumption of this book is that women's cinema is not 'at home' in any of the host cinematic or national discourses it inhabits, but that it is always an inflected mode, incorporating, reworking and contesting the conventions of established traditions. All of the films I will discuss can be situated within at least one other context (such as a national cinema, or an international mode of representation) besides that of women's cinema; few of them, however, are fully comprehended by their other contexts. A concomitant assumption of the book is that neither the makers nor the viewers of these films are exhaustively defined by their membership of the category 'women'. It has often been argued that the conceptualisation of women's cultural production as distinct from men's is counter-productive both for feminism, with its egalitarian goals, and for the individual artist who may aspire to androgynous creativity. On the other hand, it has been pointed out that artists are social subjects whatever their aspirations to the contrary, and that only the most conservative of feminisms approaches the goal of equality via the denial of social differences. The debate about the grounds for defining women's collectivity, and the political effects of doing so, is an extremely complex one, beyond the scope of this book. The fact that there is a debate, however, and that it results from the collective work of several generations of feminists, certainly militates against the dismissal of the concept of women's cultural production. Again, Deleuze's understanding of the effects of the experience of marginalisation is useful here: 'Sometimes the minority film-maker finds himself [sic] in the impasse described by Kafka: the impossibility of not "writing", the impossibility of writing in the dominant language, the impossibility of writing differently' (Deleuze 1989: 217) and behind this, 'a double impossibility, that of forming a group *and* that of not forming a group' (219). The distinctiveness of women's film-making is therefore not based on an essentialist understanding of gendered subjectivity, but on the position – or positions – of women in contemporary culture, in Kafka's impasse: neither included within nor excluded from cultural tradition, lacking a cohesive collective identity, but yet not absolutely differentiated from each other...

The themes of the chapters that follow – genre in mainstream Hollywood cinema, authorship in experimental cinema, and the politics of location in (for want of a better term) world cinema – reflect a number of considerations, including the patterns of development evident in women's cinema and important issues in the academic literature around it. Chapter 1 takes as its starting point the ways that Hollywood, a conservative popular cinema, uses genre to manage change. Women film-makers, particularly in the last decade, have taken a revisionist approach to established genres, exploiting their social and historical responsiveness to illuminate contemporary cultural concerns (Lane 2000: 55). In Chapter 2, I discuss the ways that authorship, an intensely problematic category for women who have been cast by aesthetic tradition as muses, models and medusas, has been remodelled in experimental film. Women film-makers have employed the reflexive and autobiographical modes characteristic of experimental film to construct themselves as authors, but also to throw into question the integrity of subjectivity and the stability of the self. In Chapter 3, questions of location, of *where* film-makers speak from, and how this shapes their practice, are discussed. These are germane to all films, and perhaps to Hollywood films above all, but have been most fully addressed in relation to particular practices where national and cultural identity have been consciously considered rather than taken for granted: in national film movements, post-colonial cinemas and exilic and diasporic practices.

In seeking to strike a balance between detailed textual analysis and a general overview, each chapter offers a series of thumbnail analyses rather than exhaustive readings of films. Many of the films discussed have been chosen because they are part of the canon of women's cinema, and in these cases I have made reference to more detailed analyses where they exist. In the case of films which are less well known, and may not be easily viewed, I have included more coverage of plot and style. More than twenty years ago, Mulvey wrote: 'It is hard, as yet, to speak of a feminist film-making practice. Women film-makers are few and far between' (1979: 9). Now that this is no longer the case, a book like this one can only begin to indicate the scope of women's cinema, leaving out more than it includes.

1   GIRLS' OWN STORIES: GENRE AND GENDER IN HOLLYWOOD CINEMA

Women in Hollywood: a brief historical overview

In 2001, stickers appeared at the Sundance Festival and the Academy Awards ceremony, bearing slogans such as 'THE US SENATE IS MORE PROGRESSIVE THAN HOLLYWOOD. FEMALE SENATORS: 9% FEMALE DIRECTORS: 4%' and 'THE ANATOMICALLY CORRECT OSCAR: HE'S WHITE AND MALE, JUST LIKE THE GUYS WHO WIN!' (over a picture of a corpulent statuette with a penis). One sticker lists the leading distributors who released one film directed by a woman in 2000 (Miramax, New Line, Artisan, Sony Screen Gems, Paramount Classics), and those who released none (Fine Line, Dimension, USA Films, Shooting Gallery). The stickers were the work of a group of filmmakers calling themselves Alice Locas, an offshoot of the Guerrilla Girls, an organisation of women artists which stages high-profile feminist cultural protests while wearing gorilla masks, to conceal their identities.[1] Behind this witty protest lay frustration that more than thirty years of feminism had not had more impact on Hollywood, a major industry which dominates not only US culture, but also world culture.

Things were very different in the early years of the cinema. Alice Guy, credited with directing the first narrative fiction film in 1896, emigrated from France to the US in 1907. In her working life she directed hundreds of films, 22 of them features, and owned and ran a studio, Solax. Lois

Weber, who also owned a studio, made over a hundred films, including many features, typified by their moral stance on social issues of the day. Anthony Slide (1996) documents the existence of over a dozen other female directors in the silent era, while the Women Film Pioneers Project, based at Duke University, lists sixty US pioneers, most of them directors, on its website.[2] The difference in the status and numbers of women in mainstream film production before and after the coming of sound is intriguing as well as depressing. Gerald Peary comments that 'Alice [Guy] Blaché's secret was to make her mark in film before the barriers against women came into existence, indeed before there was such a thing as a film industry' (1977: 139).

Women's involvement in the movies was a natural extension of their involvement in the theatre, and was particularly valued by those who sought to establish the respectability of the new art: films directed by women, shown in theatres managed by women, it was reasoned, were more likely to attract women and children into the audience. By the time the transition to sound was complete, most of these women directors' careers had ended, often despite their ambitions to the contrary. Although there was nothing intrinsically patriarchal in the development of sound in the cinema (in fact Alice Guy made early experiments in sound film), it resulted in an industry shake-out which adversely affected the careers of many personnel of both sexes. Slide is unable to fully explain why women directors in particular suffered such losses, although he hypothesises that unionisation may have been one of the causes. It seems likely that the enormous expense of the industry's conversion to sound and the industrial and financial reorganisation it occasioned intensified the gender bias of wider society.

In the studio era and the period immediately following, historians and critics have identified only two women directors with coherent bodies of work to their names: Dorothy Arzner and Ida Lupino (see Johnston 1975; Mayne 1994; Kuhn 1995). Arzner began her directorial career in 1927, after working in the industry as a typist, scriptwriter and editor. She worked through the 1930s, establishing a reputation as a competent professional – though not a canonised auteur outside feminist criticism – and made her last film, *First Comes Courage*, in 1943. Lupino had a successful career an actress in Hollywood B movies, before setting up as an independent to produce, write and direct low-budget films with controversial themes (including rape, bigamy, disability and unmarried motherhood). Between 1949 and 1953 she made six films, with a further and final production in 1966. Although the reconfiguration of the US film industry occurred at the height of the women's movement, New Hollywood has proved itself barely more open to female talent than the old. In addition, alternative (though still male-dominated) outlets for that talent have appeared since the end of vertical integration in 1948: television and independent/avant-garde film.[3] In 1999, women directed only four per cent of the top grossing 100 Hollywood films. The numbers of female producers, writers and editors are better, but still very low: 'Overall, women comprised 17% of all executive producers, producers, directors, writers, cinematographers, and editors working on the top 250 domestic grossing films of 1999. This figure remains unchanged from 1998' (Lauzen 2000). The apparent contradiction between these statistics and the perception sometimes expressed of a considerable increase in the number of women directing in Hollywood (see Cook 1998: 243–5) can be explained in two ways. The statistics focus on top-grossing product, the 'event movies' privileged by the economy of New Hollywood, whereas women directors tend to be assigned to 'non-event' movies with mid-range budgets and unfashionable generics (Lane 2000: 37). In addition, given that as few as fourteen films were directed by only seven women in mainstream Hollywood between 1949 and 1979, the increased numbers of the last decade not only look like but actually constitute exponential growth, while falling far short of equality.

Genre and gender: the woman's film and beyond

In the studio era, Hollywood managed the problem of accommodating a massive share of the audience, despite its non-representation in most of the key roles played by the creative workforce, by developing specialised generics and modes of address. The most obvious of these is the woman's film, a category which crosses a number of other genres, and which is defined by the presence of a central female protagonist and a concern with specifically feminine problems and experiences (for instance *Stella*

Dallas (1937), *Leave Her to Heaven* (1945) and *The Reckless Moment*
(1949)). The woman's film is marked by stylistic and narrative distortions
which result from the irreconcilability of Hollywood's ostensible moral
values and aesthetic conventions with the provision of escapist entertainment for women:

> The woman's film operated out of a paradox. It both held women
> in social bondage and released them into a dream of potency and
> freedom ... If it is true, as many suggest, that Hollywood films
> repressed women and sought to teach them what they ought to do,
> then it is equally clear that, in order to achieve this, the movies first
> had to bring to life the opposite of their own morality. To convince
> women that marriage and motherhood were the right path, movies
> had to show women making the mistake of doing something else
> ... In asking the question, What should a woman do with her life?
> they created the possibility of an answer different from the one
> they intended to provide at the end of the movie. (Basinger 1994:
> 6–7)[4]

Several scholars hypothesise a link between the woman's film and the
Production Code, which regulated Hollywood morality/ideology from the
mid-1930s to the mid-1960s. Patricia White suggests that prior to the insti-
tution of the Code, the term 'women's pictures' was applied to racy urban
sex pictures, and that the Production Code Administration attempted to
'clean up' the genre by re-imposing Victorian sexual ideology (with surprising results (1999: 20)). Steve Neale argues similarly that the Code's
pronouncements on sexuality opposed the modernity of the New Woman
with nineteenth-century values: 'Just as the Production Code also functioned, nevertheless, as a public statement of the ideological principles
Hollywood claimed to uphold, so the Cult of True Womanhood remained,
in modified form, a point of reference for Hollywood and the woman's film
a major site of its exploration' (Neale 2000: 195). Although the contemporary Hollywood 'chick flick' shares some of the features and concerns of
the classic woman's film, Neale notes that the term itself disappeared with
the Code in the 1960s, just as second-wave feminism arrived.

The woman's film emerged in the context of a wider incorporation and construction – of women's perceived tastes and interests. Patricia Mellencamp observes the centrality of romance to Hollywood's output, and its profound cultural impact:

> [Hollywood] narrative is usually a story of romance, no matter what the genre, director, studio or year. The one-hundred years dominance of this story of the couple coupling has had cumulative significance, and, I would argue, major cultural impact. For Hollywood has created the story many little girls and women believe they must make of their lives. (1995a: 24)

She suggests that romance draws women into the family by constructing sexuality as a lure which vanishes when the couple is brought together at the film's close, 'made in the fade'. Importantly, she also notes that the standard accounts of Hollywood film form and style have overlooked the determining effect of social constructions of gender, race and age on technique: 'The continuity style represents (and has created) a double standard of gender, race and age, with different conventions of lighting, make-up, speech and even action for men and women' (24). One example she gives is the differing function of the close-up for male and female stars: for the former, it shows character, for the latter, beauty. Unlike the male star, the female star requires plenty of make-up and special lighting arrangements and lenses to diffuse the light. 'The lighting apparatus it takes to achieve this is significant. It necessitates that women not move' (31), she notes, offering a technical determinant to add to the already overdetermined immobility of women in classical narrative film. By showing how thoroughly the precepts of popular romance have been assimilated by US film, Mellencamp adroitly demonstrates the extent to which the classical Hollywood cinema is, in fact, romantic.

The conventions of romance can, in turn, be contextualised in the history of sexuality and gender relations, and Hollywood's involvement in their construction. Early cinema historians have documented the significance of cinema in the articulation of a historical shift from a homosocial public sphere in nineteenth-century America to a heterosocial one in the twentieth century (see Peiss 1986; Hansen 1991). By extension, the existence of the woman's film and Hollywood's other gendered genres suggests a history of crises in heterosociality, matched only by the anxiety provoked by the spectre of a sexualised homosociality. More recent events, for instance the Clarence Thomas/Anita Hill case, and the debates around 'political correctness', indicate that the terms on which a heterosocial public sphere might function remain far from settled. Viewed as a technology of gender, to use Teresa de Lauretis's term, Hollywood cinema appears not as a stable embodiment of a consistent ideology but as an unstable hegemony within which images of egalitarian heterosexuality are almost as rare as those of contented homosexuality.

The history of women's cinema in Hollywood can be mapped in terms of its ambivalent relationship with the woman's film, its excursions into other genres, and its modifications of the ways that gender relations are constructed by particular generics. If genre is the system by which Hollywood manages change, balancing difference and standardisation, then it is also the means by which women have succeeded in introducing new perspectives and new material. Through brief analyses of a selection of films spanning the twentieth century, I hope to show how women filmmakers have used genre to work within and around the historical restrictions of Hollywood.

Protofeminists: Alice Guy and Dorothy Arzner

Alice Guy's career ended before the woman's picture came into existence. Guy worked in most of the genres of her day, including the western, and was insistent that the tasks involved in filmmaking were 'as suitable, as fascinating and as remunerative to a woman as to a man' (Guy 1996: 142). While there is no obvious feminist content in her work and she did not espouse the cause of women's suffrage (although Solax was unusual in not producing anti-suffragette films), the modernity and energy of many of her female characters relates them more closely to the New Woman of the 1890s–1920s and the active heroines of the serial queen melodramas than to the neurasthenic household angels of the nineteenth century.

The short comedy, *A House Divided* (1913), is a gentle send-up of the sentimental ideal of middle-class marriage. The house of the title is the home of an office worker and his wife, and it is divided by unfounded suspicions of infidelity on both parts, caused by a pair of man's gloves left behind by a tradesman and perfume spilled on the man's lapel by a travelling salesman. The couple argue and visit their lawyer who provides them with an agreement to communicate only via written notes. Guy introduces another misunderstanding to resolve the first: the maid is locked out during a party, and attempts to re-enter via the cellar. Thinking that they are being burgled, the woman fetches a gun which the man pulls on the maid. In the ensuing laughter, everything is explained.

The film is a matrix of divisions and continuities along the lines of class and gender. Its locations, which include the office where the man works, the dining room, kitchen and parlour of the house, and the office of the couple's lawyer, shift and alternate between the worlds of work and family, emphasising the different social roles of the characters, including women who work – the stenographer in the office and the maid in the kitchen – and women who don't – the wife, her mother and the female party guests. Across these divisions, graphic continuity creates parallels: the staging is marked by similarities of composition which rhyme the position and demeanour of the female characters from shot to shot. The film's second shot shows the husband at his desk on one side of the screen, back-to-back with the stenographer, who steals the scene with a gum-chewing, eye-rolling, scowling performance. Although comically eccentric and madly coiffed, the stenographer is also dramatically and socially significant: her forthright deflection of the perfume salesman, and assertiveness when it's time for 'home and me beau' contrast with the silliness of the central couple. Moreover, the film's first audience might have contained many female office workers like this character. Subsequent shots position the maid and the wife in the exact same portion of the screen as the stenographer, engaged in activities which involve similar gestures: the maid rolling pastry and the wife playing the piano, encouraging the spectator to see parallels and contrasts between the women.

FIGURE 1 *A House Divided*

This system of class comparisons intersects with the film's other main compositional system which involves the division of space on the lines of gender into 'his and hers', both within the frame and throughout the diegesis. The screen is often bisected in some way, by a doorframe, for instance, creating distinct spaces for male and female characters. At the party, the men separate from the women to play cards, following bourgeois social convention. At the film's end, two mentor figures reinforce the impression of male and female territory: the wife's sympathetic mother and the lawyer, who objects to the breaking of the agreement. The comedy of misunderstanding here arises from the confusion of a world in transition, from the sexual segregation of the nineteenth century to the integration of the twentieth (bringing women – and therefore perfume salesmen – into offices, for instance). In view of its brisk and feisty working women (and remembering that Guy trained as a stenographer and began her career in film as Léon Gaumont's secretary) it is hard not to conclude that the film's gentle joke is on the middle-class couple, the 'idle white woman' in Mellencamp's phrase (1995a: 196) and the childlike

FIGURE 2 *A House Divided*

husband who lends weight to the assertion made in the first intertitle of
Lois Weber's *The Blot* (1921): 'Men Are Only Boys Grown Tall.'

The paradox of Dorothy Arzner's career is that while she has come
to represent a heroic example of a woman in a man's world, her chosen
milieu, in life and in art, was that of women. The notion of the woman's
film had gained currency by the time she established her directing career,
and its effect on her work was a mixed blessing, as Judith Mayne has
observed:

> The emergence of a woman director and a genre known as the
> woman's film at approximately the same time provides a safe,
> stereotypical way to channel any challenge that Arzner might rep-
> resent whether as a woman – period – or as a woman who did not
> resemble the Hollywood ideal of femininity. (Mayne 1994: 54)

Despite this, her positioning as a woman's director allowed for 'the kind
of complex collaboration that would characterise the best aspects of

Arzner's career, that between woman director and woman writer, as well as that between director and actress' (54). If Arzner's films are examples of the genre which Molly Haskell links to 'wet, wasted afternoons' (1973: 155), many of them are atypically cheerful, portraying female friendships and communities which reflect the productive working collaborations Arzner enjoyed with actresses such as Clara Bow and writers such as Zoe Akins, and perhaps also her committed relationship with choreographer Marion Morgan.

Arzner's work has been a touchstone in feminist criticism since the early 1970s, and has been interpreted by different critics as a precursor to feminist counter-cinema (Johnston 1975), an example of Hollywood's ability to recuperate women's discourse (Suter 1988), and an instance of lesbian authorship (Mayne 1994). When Arzner's work was rediscovered in the 1970s, critics emphasised its discontinuity. Haskell comments on 'the jerky unpredictability of a vision not quite resolved into a style' which, in her view, expresses 'the discomfort of a woman who feels herself an artist in an alien land'.[5] Johnston argues that the 'disjointed and fragmented' narratives of Arzner's films result from the contestation of the dominant, patriarchal discourse of Hollywood by Arzner's feminine discourse:

> In Arzner's films it is the universe of the male which invites scrutiny, which is rendered strange ... It is only the discourse of the woman, and her desire for transgression, which provides the principle of coherence and generates knowledge, and it is in the woman that Arzner locates the possibility of truth within the film text. It is also for this reason that the narrative appears quite disjointed and fragmented; the conventions of plot and development are quite fully in evidence, but the work of the woman's discourse renders the narrative strange, subverting and dislocating it at the level of meaning. (Johnston 1975: 6)

Johnston's reading of Arzner's films through the 1970s vogue for defamiliarisation and reflexivity raised *Dance, Girl, Dance* (1940) to the status of a feminist classic. The film tells the story of two friends, Bubbles (Lucille Ball) and Judy (Maureen O'Hara), who work together in a dance troupe but

nurture seemingly opposite desires, for artistic self-expression and commercial gain. When Bubbles becomes a vaudeville star, she creates a role
for Judy as her stooge, interrupting the former's striptease with a classical
ballet, to the infuriation of the audience. Exasperated, Judy stops the show
with an angry speech which perfectly describes the gendered economy
of looking and money which circumscribes the women's performances:
'Fifty cents for the privilege of staring at a girl the way your wife won't let
you ... We'd laugh right back at the lot of you, only we're paid to let you
sit there and roll your eyes and make your screamingly clever remarks.'
Johnston judges this moment to be a rupture in the film's fabric, the only
completely 'decisive *break* effected between the dominant discourse and
the discourse of the woman' in Arzner's work (6). Judy's return of the male
gaze and her accompanying critique of women's objectification seem to
prefigure feminist film theory's sexual politics of the look.

However, as Judith Mayne has shown, this argument is made at the cost
of the dismissal of Arzner's lesbianism and the suppression of its textual
traces. Mayne points out that the dancers are also the objects of female
gazes, notably those of Madame Basilova, the head of the dance troupe,
and the secretary of the director of the ballet company which Judy wants
to join. The latter leads the applause which follows Judy's angry speech.
The former is seen gazing tenderly (even 'longingly' (Mayne 1994: 144)) at
Judy as she rehearses, and Mayne hypothesises that Basilova (changed
from a man, 'Basiloff', in the script), is as close as Arzner comes to authorial self-inscription: Basilova shares Arzner's style of dress, as a classic
'butch', as well as the profession of her longtime companion, Morgan.
These female gazes are not located within any explicit or even implicit
lesbian scenarios, but they are situated within a world of homosociality
which dominates the film:

I have noted that, frequently in Arzner's films, the development of
heterosexual romance intrudes upon all-female worlds, and that
while the films often conclude with the requisite happy couple,
such conclusions seem somewhat fragile in regard to the amount
of time and energy devoted, screen-wise, to the female worlds.
(Mayne 1994: 131)

Arzner uses dance dialectically to represent the women's economic and sexual dilemmas: Bubbles dances to attract men, performing stereotypical female sexuality; Judy dances for artistic self-expression, attracting a man incidentally (insofar as such a thing could ever be incidental in a Hollywood film) but both are ultimately in pursuit of money and social mobility. Moreover, as Mayne points out, the two styles are synthesised in the rehearsal of the American Ballet Company, which segues from traditional ballet into vibrant modern dance incorporating street styles. Judy is shown watching in admiration as a dancer who resembles Bubbles performs centre-stage: through the friendship of Bubbles and Judy, the film suggests a possible rapprochement between high and low art forms. Despite its conventional ending with the formation of two couples, Mayne argues that *Dance, Girl, Dance* presents heterosexual romance ironically, inscribing it within a patriarchal *economy*. Mayne's reading of Arzner's films revises earlier accounts, but does not, in my view, altogether invalidate them. Patricia White's (1999) notion of the 'femme' film in which homosociality functions as a condition which might or might not, depending partly on the historical viewing situation, bring lesbianism to view, seems wholly appropriate to the tissue of homosociality, feminism and lesbian desire in Arzner's work.

Genre meets art: Girlfriends and Love Letters

Claudia Weill's *Girlfriends* (1978) belongs to a small group of films which revisit the woman's picture from the perspective of 1970s feminism. It was made independently with arts funding and distributed by Warner Bros. Institutionally, it belongs in the tradition of the independently-made *Easy Rider* (1969), as well as anticipating the more experimental independent features made by New York feminists in the 1980s, such as *Born in Flames* (Lizzie Borden, 1983), *Variety* (Bette Gordon, 1984) and *She Must Be Seeing Things* (Sheila McLaughlin, 1987). Thematically, *Girlfriends* answers Haskell's call for on-screen female camaraderie to parallel the male buddy movie initiated by *Easy Rider* and its travelling companions in the 1960s (1973: 371). In an episodic, de-dramatised narrative mode, the film follows the progress of Susan (Melanie Mayron), a young

Jewish photographer in New York City, over an eighteen-month period, beginning when her roommate, Anne (Anita Skinner), a WASP writer, moves out to get married and start a family. The differences between the choices made by the two women are played up, for their own sake and to heighten the sense of the difficulty of maintaining the friendship. Anne finds it hard to continue work or studies after she has a child. Despite her economic security, she decides to terminate a subsequent pregnancy in the hope of pursuing a career as a writer. Susan struggles with money problems but gets her first show, and begins to establish herself as a photographer. Her love life, consisting of a flirtation with a middle-aged married rabbi, a shaky relationship with a solipsistic young man, and an unwelcome sexual advance from a woman who briefly shares her apartment, falters between pathos and bathos. The film's themes relate it to middle-class 'lifestyle' feminism, and, according to Christine Geraghty, coincide with a stable pattern of concerns in the woman's film of the 1970s, which include, in order of priority: 'the problem of relationships with men, the importance of friendships between women and, though this comes a poor third, the difficulties of combining these things with holding down a job' (1986: 144–5). Annette Kuhn describes this entanglement with the priorities of romance in terms of a structural organisation with sexual implications. The film, she argues, is open-ended because 'full closure is perhaps impossible, given the nature of the structuring enigmas of the narrative':

> Resolution in *Girlfriends* might be brought about by the establishment of love relationships for both Anne and Susan: either with each other, or with new partners. Although the first option would fit in well with the structural demands of classic narrative, as well as with the powerful 'romance' model, its content is excluded by rules, conscious and unconscious, currently governing representations of homosexuality in dominant cinema. (1982: 137)

The alternative, an ending in which both women are happily coupled, would undermine the buddy structure, as well as defying credibility 'caught in its own contradictions, the narrative cannot be resolved in the classic manner' (137). The film not only bypasses the possibility of a lesbian relationship, but goes out of its way to dismiss it, with the introduction of Ceil, the 'free spirit' and temporary roommate who annoys Susan by borrowing her clothes and rearranging her things, as well as making a pass at her. Ceil is included in the film because 'Weill feels she must introduce and dismiss lesbianism to clarify the fact that Susan experiences profound love for her friend in an asexual way', but with the unfortunate effect of reinforcing homophobia (Fischer 1989: 240). *Girlfriends* illustrates one of the paradoxical challenges which 1970s feminism faced: the climate of 'sexual liberation' made open discourse on homosexuality possible for the first time, literally in the case of the film industry, where explicit representation of gay and lesbian characters was permitted only after the abolition of the Production Code, but it also intensified the effects of heterosexist ideology. The possibility of openly distinguishing lesbian romance from female friendship is registered by *Girlfriends* as an invidious necessity which undermines the female solidarity implied by its ambiguous title.

Like the buddy movies *Butch Cassidy and the Sundance Kid* (1969) and *Thelma and Louise* (1991), *Girlfriends* ends with a freeze-frame: a purely formal ending necessitated by the impossibility of reconciling the rhythm and repetition of the buddy movie with the climax and closure of Hollywood narrative. The final scene, one of the film's too infrequent moments of intimacy between the two women, concludes with the arrival of Anne's husband. As she goes to him, the frame freezes with Susan in a moment of solitude, recomposing her expression to conceal her disappointment at this intrusion. The freeze frame ending is especially typical of a short-lived tendency in American cinema through the 1970s, described by Thomas Elsaesser as a 'new realism' in conflict with the storytelling traditions of Hollywood: 'a formal search for a film narrative free from the parasitic and synthetic causality of a dramaturgy of conflict … a mode of representation that validates the real without encasing it in the categories of the symbolic and the spectacular' (Elsaesser 1975: 15). Although Elsaesser's essay focuses on male auteurs and genres, it casts an interesting sidelight on *Girlfriends*, revealing its significant strengths as well as the source of its weaknesses. Geraghty points out that the film 'is a naturalist work in the sense that it relies for much of its effect on the accumulation of surface detail', and notes the striking simplicity of its camerawork (1986: 138). The emphasis on character rather than story, the de-dramatised and elliptical narration and the accretion of everyday detail, rendered with almost ethnographic verisimilitude, affiliate the film to the brief efflorescence of a minimalist American art cinema described by Elsaesser, in terms remarkably consonant with those of the feminism of the time, as 'a revaluation of the real on the far side of either fetishistic fixation or conceptual abstraction' (19). The film's many domestic scenes give substance to its otherwise schematic treatment of the women's choices – the shifting rivalry and respect between Susan and Anne's husband Martin is handled delicately, as is Anne's ambivalence about motherhood, most noticeably in the scenes dealing with her pregnancy and abortion. Nevertheless, there is nothing in the film that comes close to the hyperrealist minimalism of Chantal Akerman's *Jeanne Dielman, 23 Quai du Commerce, 1080 Bruxelles* (1975), with its obsessively close observation of a woman's gestures in a domestic setting. Like the westerns and road movies Elsaesser discusses, *Girlfriends* remains rooted in the generic and narrational norms of the US mainstream, on which it depends for its audience: 'The innovatory line in the American cinema can be seen to progress not via conceptual abstraction but by *shifting and modifying traditional genres and themes, while never quite shedding their support*' (Elsaesser 1975: 18, my emphasis). Lucy Fischer notes the presence of reflexive systems in the film which, she argues, situate it in 'the gap between experimental and classical modes,' (1989: 249) subtly broaching issues of vision and representation without alienating a popular audience. These systems involve Susan's photographs, her encounters with the worlds of art and the media, and, on one occasion, her spectacles. However, although Fischer's argument is convincing, the systems themselves do not add much depth to the film. Susan's photographs, for instance, which are mostly depictions of families at weddings and barmitzvahs, provide an ironic contrast to her single status, but beyond this, do not interact dynamically with anything in the narrative or mise-en-scène.

Girlfriends was produced in a period when auteur-directors working at the edges of the mainstream hoped to create a popular art cinema by attenuating and disconnecting the generic and narrative conventions of Hollywood without actively reworking them. Weill's film reveals two ways in which this is a problematic strategy for feminist cinema: the retention of an established generic and narrative architecture makes it difficult to develop new subject matter, such as female friendship, while what is lost in the partial disengagement from a model which revolved around intense passion and vigorous action is the affirmative dimension of clas-sical dramaturgy, the belief in the capacity of people to effect changes in the worlds they inhabit which is one of the few values which Hollywood has in common with feminism.

Throughout the 1980s, women filmmakers working in the low-budget independent sector expressed increasingly mainstream ambitions, as, for instance, in Bette Gordon's statement: 'My work is in the mainstream, but I insert questions and discomfort into images, narratives and stories. Other filmmakers are interested in creating a separate or alternative femi-nist erotics. I am not, since that alternative suggests marginality – the "other place" outside of culture that women have already been assigned. I don't want to maintain that outsideness' (1984: 194). Returning the compliment, Hollywood modernised its output by assimilating artistic strategies – and personnel – from alternative cinema.

Love Letters (1983) directed by Amy Jones for Roger Corman's New World Pictures (the year after making her directing debut with *Slumber Party Massacre*), is a revisionist woman's film produced by an exploitation com-pany with upmarket ambitions and a surprising reputation for feminism. High artistic aspirations are signalled by art-world references as glaring as product placements: the title sequence shows letters burning on a hot-plate, invoking the similar burning of photographs in Hollis Frampton's avant-garde classic *(nostalgia)* (1971); John Berger's *Permanent Red* appears as a coffee table book; Walter Benjamin's famous essay 'The Work of Art in the Age of Mechanical Reproduction' comes up in conver-sation. The inclusion of a clip from *From Here to Eternity* (1953) and a photographer as a leading character seem to betoken reflexivity (without actually functioning as such). A counter-cultural ambience is evoked by the Venice Beach locations, and explicit sex scenes with echoes of *Last Tango in Paris* (1975) imbue the film with New World's ethos of sexual libertarianism. These conflicting generic orientations are held together by a more or less conventional woman's film narrative: while arranging the affairs of her much-loved late mother, the protagonist, Anna Winter (Jamie Lee Curtis), discovers some old love letters written to her mother by the secret love of her life. In an attempt to recreate this romance, Anna starts seeing an older married man, Oliver Andrews (James Keach), a patron of the small radio station where she works as a DJ. After the affair ends badly, Anna has a graveside encounter with her mother's lover, and admits to him that she has never experienced a love of the kind he had with her mother.

The narrative is structured by three eternal triangles, made up of Anna and her parents, Anna's parents and the mother's lover, and Anna, Oliver and his wife. An early scene shows Anna at her dying mother's bedside with a gift of gardenias (the flowers which, we later discover, her lover used to give her). Anna's affection for her mother is contrasted with her feelings for her father: his arrival breaks up the women's intimacy, and Anna leaves, taking care not to touch him. Bereavement and the discovery of her mother's infidelity have a catalytic effect on her dislike of him, which the film motivates by characterising him as a shabby, embittered alcoholic. This sketch of unresolved Oedipal tensions lays the ground for Anna's attempt to recreate her mother's affair, aspiring to be like her, but also to be like the lover: she wears her mother's opal ring, a gift from the lover, but also uses phrases from his letters when she speaks and writes to Oliver. A dream sequence towards the end of the film anchors her shifting identifications in a violent variant on the primal scene fantasy (i.e. the fantasy of one's origins in parental intercourse). In the sequence, Anna, in her nightdress, comes down the stairs of the family home to find her parents arguing loudly. A shot from the parents' point of view shows Anna played by a child actor instead of Curtis. Recycling a line from earlier in the film, the father says: 'You're so like her', as he points a gun at her. The child takes the gun from him and shoots him. The next sequence, showing Anna startled awake by the sound, is identical to the film's pre-credit sequence, except that in the first instance, the sound is explained as the banging of an unsecured window rather than a gunshot. Bracketed in this way, the bulk of the narrative assumes a status analogous to the dream sequence in that its function is the working out of an unconscious problem. The film's construction of Anna's unconscious desires is contradictory: she wants to be like her mother, she wants to have her mother to herself, and, in line with Freud's family romance theory, she wants a different, better father – perhaps one more appropriate to her professional status and high cultural interests. Animated by these conflicting identifications, her narrative function oscillates between the active and passive modes of investigation and sexual objectification, or superimposes one on the other in a mise-en-scène which is doubled by her – and our – perception of one relationship in terms of another. Despite the generic difference, Curtis's role in *Love Letters* reverberates with the gender ambiguity of the horror film 'Final Girl' persona for which she was best known in the early 1980s (see Clover 1992).

The working out of female Oedipal problems in *Love Letters* appears symptomatic of the individualistic version of feminism which gained currency in the 1980s (as well as allegorising the conditions of its own production, in the mismatch of Jones' artistic aims and Corman's pragmatism): the ambitious young woman seeks in her father both a prototype object for her heterosexual desire and a role model relevant to her professional aspirations. Finding her actual father unsuitable on both counts, Anna explores the possibility of finding symbolic replacements for him, but her combination of traditionally male and female Oedipal identifications, predisposing her to aggression against a couple *and* victimisation within one, leads to an impasse. The generic context of *Love Letters* has much to do with this outcome: a romantic woman's picture updated by its sexual explicitness, it defines the field in which the character must function as the realm of emotions and heterosexual relations. The active drive which the protagonist gains from masculine identification is manifest only in the most negative ways: in rivalry, jealousy and voyeurism. The scenes in which Anna follows Oliver's wife and daughter to the park and provokes a fight by spying on the family in their home bear a discomforting resemblance to the decade's anti-feminist high-water mark: *Fatal Attraction* (1987). The film's only gesture towards gender solidarity is the inclusion of a down-to-earth best friend, Wendy (Amy Madigan), but the romance plot necessarily sidelines the female buddy. The gun in Anna's dream suggests another generic horizon for the male-identified woman, ruled by the codes of action rather than those of passion. This possibility is taken up in Kathryn Bigelow's *Blue Steel* (1990), which – surely not by coincidence – reunites the most distinctive elements of Jones' film – Curtis, a weak and violent father, and a gun – in the context of a psychological thriller.

Towards a women's action cinema: Blue Steel

Hollywood's flirtation with art cinema was short-lived, and in the restabilised economic environment of the 1980s the industry made a 'return to genre filmmaking ... now marked by greater self-consciousness' (Smith 1998: 11). At the same time, independent filmmaking was transformed from an oppositional practice to an apprenticeship for the mainstream. Kathryn Bigelow is the most successful of a number of directors who crossed from counter-cinema into Hollywood in the 1980s and 1990s (see Lane 2000). She began making action pictures at about the same time as feminist film theorists began re-evaluating popular genres previously regarded as repositories of the most uncomplicated masculinism. Mulvey and Johnston's theorisations of women's absence from Hollywood cinema were historicised by the discovery of new logics of gender in contemporary films, involving ambiguous figurations of masculinity and femininity and complex cross-gender identifications on the part of spectators (see Clover 1992; Tasker 1993). Much of this work is concerned with cinema as public fantasy, and with the ingenuity of the audience rather than that of the filmmakers; Bigelow's work stands out in this context, because its play with the conventions of genre and gender is the consciously experimental work of a woman director.

Far from being a film about women's involvement in police work, *Blue Steel* is, as Yvonne Tasker claims, 'a complex, psychological thriller which attempts to explore the role of women in the action cinema' (1993: 147). Most of the critical writing on the film takes the form of textual exegesis, tracing the convoluted ramifications of the heroine's assumption of the conventionally masculine police uniform and gun. However, its reflexivity leaves little room for sub-textual discoveries. In this, it may be part of a trend, remarked upon by Mellencamp: 'Because we believed in the 1970s that the Hollywood movie worked through concealment, a strategy akin to women's masquerade, it became our job to reveal its working, to look beneath the surface ... But culture operates differently today, telling us up front what it is doing, hiding its work right in front of our eyes' (1995a: 45). With an airless stylisation which announces an overriding concern with aesthetics, the film's opening sequences offer an almost schematic overview of its themes, organised in relation to its principal motifs, the gun and the uniform. The film starts, in typical Hollywood style, *in medias res*, with Megan Turner (Curtis) in police uniform attending the scene of a violent domestic dispute. This turns out to be a training exercise, at which she fails because she mistakes the woman for a victim rather than a perpetrator. 'You killed the husband, but the wife killed you,' says the trainer, 'in the field you've got to have eyes in the back of your head.' As well as foreshadowing subsequent plot developments, including the domestic violence between Megan's parents, from which she wants to save her mother, and the murder from which she fails to save her best friend Tracy, the scene warns the audience against making conventional assumptions about the gendering of violence (a warning which is unfortunately irrelevant to all but one of the film's characters). The trainer's words identify the deficit which her progress through the film will make good: by developing an uncanny sympathy with her enemy, she will, by the third act, be able to sense his presence as if she had eyes in the back of her head. The theme of gun fetishism is introduced next, in the credit sequence, which consists of hyperreal extreme close-ups of a police handgun, bathed in blue light.

As Tasker notes, the 'obvious pleasure' which the film takes in gun fetishism, and which it invites the audience to share, complicates its stance on gendered violence (1993: 159). A connection is forged between gun fetishism and the fetishisation of the female form, as the placing of the gun in a holster segues into the next sequence, in which Megan/Curtis is seen dressing for her graduation ceremony. The juxtaposition of a white lacy bra with a crisp blue shirt and shiny black shoes, and the ritual care with which they are put on, suggests transvestism (although this is, presumably, a woman's uniform). As the film progresses, the police uniform becomes emblematic of Megan's contested identity, variously signifying power and authority, complicity with patriarchal law, phallic sexual objectification and, in a lighter moment, 'butch' lesbian appeal. In three sequences, Bigelow outlines the generic field in which the film will function, and reveals the ways that ideological and actual transvestism will enable and ensnare the female hero.

Transvestism has a long history in feminist film theory, beginning with Mulvey's assertion of the masculinisation of the female spectator, dragged along 'by the scruff of the text' by films which address her as male (Mulvey 1981: 12). Queer theory's radical reassessment of drag and transvestism has transformed cross-dressing from a metaphor for the erasure of an authentic identity to the very axiom of identity as cultural construction. Needeya Islam places *Blue Steel* between these two positions, arguing that its use of transvestism to signal narrative status rather than desire offers the spectator the pleasures of masculine mobility and agency without eclipsing femininity as a cognitive position. By placing the transvestism on the screen, and problematising it there, Bigelow spares the female spectator the 'historical alternatives' of masochistic identification with passive femininity and cross-gender identification with active masculinity: 'Megan in uniform is an acknowledgement of the usual limitations placed on female spectatorship; she gives the problematic nature of identification a tactile presence' (Islam 1995: 109). The film poses transvestism as a dilemma of another kind: Megan's uniform and gun attract the fetishist psycho-killer Eugene (Ron Silver), but also offer the only means to defeat him, in the film's final shoot-out, fighting fire with fire.

Despite the interest which the film holds for psychoanalytic criticism, the conventionality of the motivation which Bigelow supplies for Megan's identification with masculine power – resistance to her violent father, prompting allegiances first with the law, and then, when its institutions reveal their corrupt paternalism, with justice – indicates that *Blue Steel* is much less concerned with psychology than it is with genre. Megan's status as active female hero is represented as the equivocal result of a continuous contest between generic conventions which would position her as victim and those which enable her to defend herself. Bigelow borrows moves from the rape-revenge drama and the horror movie, reworks conventions from the thriller and the detective movie, and invokes the myth of Oedipus which, semioticians have argued, underpins all western narrative tradition (see de Lauretis 1984: 103–57). Islam regards the semiotic play of the film as ultimately – and intentionally – unstable:

> The constant negotiation of the familiar and the unfamiliar, in establishing and disregarding gender codes, bears a significant relation to Bigelow's project in the domain of genre, where her heterodoxy makes definite, clear-cut readings impossible. This resistance to being either a faithful cop thriller or a straightforward feminist revision (which is the film's most potent critical property) exposes the difficulty of critically challenging generic expectations when to be effective requires the maintenance of some of the genre's most problematic terms (1995: 113).

Chief amongst these 'problematic terms' is the melodramatic binarism which codes difference as opposition, resulting, as many critics have noted, in the victim status of all the women in the film apart from Megan, and the mobilisation of anti-semitic stereotyping in order to define her superiority to Eugene. *Blue Steel* does not succeed in solving all the problems it sets itself – as the opening sequences tell us it will not, and perhaps does not want to. It does, however, mark the beginning of a period in which play with genre and costume have become standard feminist strategies.

Redressing cultural history: Little Women and The Ballad of Little Jo

Two distinct trends emerged in Hollywood films by women in the 1990s: period settings and gender ambiguity. These trends are united in the motif of historical cross-dressing in Maggie Greenwald's revisionist western, *The Ballad of Little Jo* (1993). Most of the decade's period films by women have been costume dramas from literary sources, such as Gillian Armstrong's *Little Women* (1994), Jane Campion's *Portrait of a Lady* (1996) and Agnieszka Holland's *Washington Square* (1997).[6] A smaller group are

FIGURE 3 *Little Women*

original stories developed from historical research, including Julie Dash's independent film, *Daughters of the Dust*, *The Ballad of Little Jo*, and Greenwald's most recent film, *Songcatcher* (1999). The ambitions of these films are specific in each case, but broadly, they include preserving and reworking women's literary traditions, re-examining the place of women in books by men, discovering or constructing analogies between past and present, and revising and re-imagining the past for its own sake. The feminist revival of the costume drama represents a response to the increased emphasis on spectacle and the targeting of highly specific audiences in 1990s cinema: redesigned for high visual impact, the revisionist costume drama shoe-horns feminist sensibility into a niche market.

Little Women and *The Ballad of Little Jo* are latter-day contributions to America's most mythic – and most gender-specific – genres: women's domestic fiction, a popular tradition of the nineteenth century, within which Louisa M. Alcott's book is a landmark, and the western, a genre associated with masculinity, and which, Jane Tompkins argues, arose in direct response to the women's novel:

This point-for-point contrast between a major popular form of the twentieth century and the major popular form of the nineteenth is not accidental. The Western *answers* the domestic novel. It is the antithesis of the cult of domesticity that dominated American Victorian culture. The Western hero, who seems to ride in and out of nowhere, in fact comes riding in out of the nineteenth century. And every piece of baggage he doesn't have, every word he doesn't say, every creed in which he doesn't believe is absent for a reason. (1992: 39)[7]

Armstrong and Greenwald's films represent two alternative feminist res-ponses to this cultural gender war, one arguing for the continuing relevance of a feminine form, the other engaging in the reworking of a masculine form, although a leaning towards synthesis rather than sepa-ratism is apparent in both, in the motif of cross-dressing, so that as well as joining dialectically opposed traditions, each of the two films points to the possibility of reconciliation.

Set in Concord, Massachusetts, around the time of the Civil War, *Little Women* has two main concerns: love among women, in a family context, and the pursuit of a vocation, preferably as a profession. It re-reads nine-teenth-century feminism with contemporary eyes ('Blast these wretched skirts!'). At the start of the film, the attraction which writing holds for Jo March (Winona Ryder) is emphatically due to its fantastic, transformative potential, and her taste runs to the gothic. By the film's conclusion with the publication of her novel, she has learned to write more soberly from what she knows. The tension between youthful fantasies of transgres-sion and disguise and mature self-abnegation is one of the structuring patterns of the film. Jo and her sisters pass their time performing plays made from her stories, and writing for their home-made newspaper. Their roles, in their plays and editorial meetings, involve much cross-dressing, which Jo throws herself into enthusiastically. The matriarch of the fam-ily, Marmee (Susan Sarandon), leads the girls in performing good works for the poor, and favours boisterous play and serious education over the corsetted leisure which was the norm of the times. Even so, Jo is slow to accept her as a role model: 'I don't know if I could ever be like Marmee. I rather crave violence. If only I could be like father and go to war and stand up to the lions of injustice.' Jo's friendship with the boy next door, who misconstrues her camaraderie as desire, is rendered as doubling by the physical likeness of the two, especially after she cuts and sells her hair. Her rejection of his proposal signals both unreadiness to leave the homo-social space of her home and emergence as a sexual subject to whom difference and desire are resolutely Oedipal. Jo hesitates on the brink of heterosexuality, understood as renunciation ('Why must we marry at all? Why can't we stay as we are?'), before choosing an older, professorial partner whose lack of virility echoes that of her wounded war veteran father, notable by his absence from most of the film. The film ends with a love scene which lasts less than three minutes and consists largely of misunderstanding, played in the cold and rain and overshadowed by the arrival of the galleys of Jo's novel.

Patricia Mellencamp reads this resolution as an acknowledgement of the attitudes of contemporary women, for whom marriage and family feature alongside, rather than in opposition to, feminism: 'Historical feminism unites with true romance, fashioning a feminism for the 1990s' (1995a: 46), although it also recalls the novels of Charlotte Brontë, where romance and freedom are reconciled by the heroine's choice of a husband who is in some way damaged or marginal by the time of the marriage if not before. Robin Swicord's screenplay and Armstrong's direction intro-duce subtle changes from the book, reducing the significance of the romance, cutting Alcott's conclusion in which Jo indefinitely defers her literary ambitions while she raises sons and runs a boys' school, and foregrounding Jo's resistance to femininity and marriage, to which she must, nevertheless, eventually succumb.

The Ballad of Little Jo is based on the bare facts of the life of Josephine Monaghan, an East Coast society girl who transformed herself into the westerner Little Jo after her family rejected her for bearing an illegitimate son. The film presents cross-dressing as a tactic of survival rather than an erotic or identity choice. At its start, Jo (Suzy Amis) heads into the West in women's clothes, where she is sold by a tinker and pursued by two would-be rapists. She hits on the idea of her protective disguise by chance, because the store she stumbles into does not stock ready-made dresses. The intercutting of her transformation in front of a mirror with her seduction by a society photographer associates cross-dressing with loss of identity and social position. The luxuriance of her red hair is empha- sised as she hacks it off, and the equation of transvestism with renuncia- tion is sealed in the gesture of scarring her face with a cut-throat razor. Two other costume changes in the film are also responses to threat: Jo makes a coat of the skins of the coyotes which initially terrorise her along with the flock of sheep she tends on the isolated hills, and she makes herself an ugly calico dress in an unfeasible attempt to retreat into femi- ninity after seeing neighbouring homesteaders massacred by the hench- men of the land-grabbing cattle company. However, despite the coerced nature of Jo's identity as a man, it is also presented as an occasional source of pleasure — hers and the spectator's — for instance, when she demonstrates her newly-acquired gun skills at a wedding celebration, or in the spine-tingling moment when her companion tells her (consoling her for the loss of her son): 'you are a free white man, and soon you will vote'. Transvestism is understood in more or less opposite ways by *Little Women* and *The Ballad of Little Jo*: in the former, it is patterned after the pre-Oedipal masculinity theorised by Freud and drawn into feminist film theory by Mulvey in her work on the western and melodrama (1981); in the latter, it is viewed as adaptive, a protective disguise and an acclimatisa- tion to harsh living conditions.

Critical debate about the depiction of Jo's Chinese male companion, 'Tinman' (David Chung) has focused on the problem of whether Green- wald effects a simple role reversal, and in doing so invokes the racist stereotype of feminised oriental masculinity (see Rich 2001). Tania Modleski argues that the film explores the historical reality beyond the stereotype, that Chinese men often did work otherwise taken by working- class women. In other ways, the patterning of difference between the two characters is more complex than wholesale reversal. A crucial shot in the film for several critics represents Jo's point of view as she looks at Tinman washing in the river stripped to the waist, which has been criticised for objectifying, even fetishising, his body. Jo's face as she gazes at his long, loose hair and toned body registers desire, but also, it can be suggested, envy of a physical freedom she has never enjoyed and regret at the loss of her own hair. As in the film's violent shoot-out, the complexity and ambiguity of feeling expressed by Amis's face modifies the conventional meaning of the point of view shot. Stella Bruzzi's distinction between between cross-dressing and androgyny provides a useful approach to the gendering of the relationship:

> Despite signalling transgression and danger, the cross-dressed or 'dragged-up' body still utilises the difference between the sexes for effect, whether through camouflage or exaggerated citation ... On the androgynous body is exacted ambiguity, the diminution of difference, and what is manifested is a softening of the contours – between corporeality and metaphor, male and female, straight and gay, real and imagined. (1997: 176)

Bruzzi classifies Little Jo and Tinman as androgynous characters, particularly in the film's seductive sex scene, with its striking symmetries and contrasts. In a mise-en-scène which emphasises texture – rough hewn timber, furry animal pelts, warm skin – Jo and Tinman help each other out of identical long underwear, his long hair counterpointing with her muscular body, both bearing scars which tell their stories: 'The man Jo falls in love with, therefore, is as feminised as she is masculinised, and both of them are androgynous. In social terms, theirs is a reciprocal bonding in which they share roles and transgress traditional gender boundaries' (183). In fact, the film deploys cross-dressing *and* androgyny: Jo masquerades as a man in public, but behaves as an androgynous woman in private. This is paralleled to an extent by Tinman's parodic assumption of the mask of servility in his role as Chinese houseboy, although his subaltern status translates into inequality in his relationship with Jo, and its coding as feminine is indicative of the difficulty of resignifying cultural *and* sexual difference.

This is a difficulty in the film, for the characters, and of the film, for Greenwald. The extent to which the relationship can be a safe haven from the oppression both characters have endured is limited by the impossibility of escaping from society. This is most clearly illustrated by the blazing row triggered by Jo's attempt to resume her femininity, when Tinman trashes the pie she has baked for him and she throws him her rifle, with the sarcastic suggestion that he might like to fight the cattle company's hired killers: in their interdependency, each is constrained by the consequences of the other's history as well as their own.

Some critics were disappointed at Little Jo's heterosexuality, but this is to misread the film's generic ambitions: although the character of Percy (Ian McKellen), whose repressed homosexual desires return as sexual violence against women, casts a sidelight on the western's reactionary homosociality, the film's real challenge to the genre is its inscription of a progressive heterosociality. One of its paradoxes, which may be a tendency in stories of women passing as men, is that it draws attention to the hardships of men's lives as much as to those of women's, and in doing so, brings compassion – although not sentimentality – into the western. Visually, this translates into a concern with the work done inside and outside the home, apparent in the camera's close attention to detail, imposing an intimacy of scale which, Modleski suggests, brings together the traditions of female domesticity and male adventure:

> It could be said that Greenwald is not countering one, male, perspective with another, female, one, but is combining them to produce a text that pushes beyond differently gendered views, inspiring in the spectator both awe at the grandeur of the landscape and a sense of the intimate pleasures of interacting with the land and its diverse inhabitants. (1999: 174)

Feminism and the chick flick: The 24 Hour Woman

The diversification of women directors into a wider variety of genres has met with unanimous approval in feminist film criticism. There is less agreement about the future of the woman's film, or its modern descendant, the chick flick, which is regarded by some as a historical 'ghetto' (see Cook 1998). Certainly, the chick flick can be a risky specialisation for a director, as Christina Lane explains:

With the rise of the conservative New Right (and its heavy emphasis on economic success), and with the Hollywood trend toward blockbusters in the 1980s and 1990s, women's genres hold a very precarious position. They may succeed because of their status as differentiated product; however, they continue to represent risky 'niche' pictures because of their failure to attract young male audiences. (2000: 66)

On the other hand, it is precisely this uncertainty, resulting from its alignment with the most unfashionable aspects of femininity, that makes the chick flick politically significant. Although the genre has several high-profile practitioners in Hollywood, including Nora Ephron and Martha Coolidge, its most creative reinvention in recent years is Nancy Savoca's independent feature, *The 24 Hour Woman* (1999). Savoca shifts the woman's film out of its melodramatic mode and into fast-paced Hawksian comedy, which provides chaos, speed and a propensity for narrative reversals altogether appropriate for her subject: what happens when women try to combine professional life and parenthood. Grace (Rosie Perez) is the workaholic producer of a cable TV morning show called 'The 24 Hour Woman'. When her accidental pregnancy is announced on air, the ratings soar and the show goes network, piling on the pressure just as she has begun to look forward to maternity leave (or 'Maternity Leave???!!!' as her female boss pronounces it).

After the birth, Grace feels torn in two directions. Savoca extracts high anxiety and slapstick comedy from a scene which ends with Grace missing her daughter's first birthday party and winding up under arrest for swearing at a police officer on the subway. Grace's husband, Eddie, a presenter on the show, considers himself a perfect new man while absenting himself whenever he wants so he can chase his big break as an action hero in Hollywood. Eventually, Grace cracks and gives him a piece of her mind at gunpoint on air, in a hysterical scene in which all but Perez are cross-dressed for a themed show ('sex switcheroo'). While Eddie cringes on the floor in nylons and heels, the suited and moustached women around him unwittingly parody their own power-dressed feminism. The film winds up to its denouèment via a series of narrative switchbacks:

FIGURE 4 *The 24 Hour Woman*

Grace tries staying home, then cashes in on her notoriety to get another show. This time she follows the example of her assistant, Madeline (Marianne Jean-Baptiste), a calm mother of three who leaves her kids each day with their father. At the end of the film, Grace and Madeline ride off in a taxi, leaving Eddie – whose cross-dressed cowardice cannot have helped his action hero prospects – pushing the buggy. Although Savoca sends up the TV show which her characters make, with its faddish mix of feminism, fitness, high-speed cookery, psychic divination and romantic advice, her film is part of the same mass-mediated flow of contradictory chatter, and because of this, it works: things turn around so many times that everything seems provisional, nothing is fixed. The characters inhabit a swirl of – mostly half-baked – ideologies, in which, although everything is not possible, some things certainly are.

The multiple dilemmas of Savoca's film touch on issues raised by most of the other films discussed in this chapter: domesticity and employment, creativity and motherhood, heterosexual romance and female friendship.

The fact that Savoca can show these dichotomies in flux, as choices which are neither permanent nor mutually exclusive, avoiding the rigid oppositions which some of the other films construct, is both a measure of the (limited) progress which has been made towards gender equality in the US over the last century, and an effect of the film's generic orientations, in women's popular culture and comedy (both of which can sustain a lot of contradiction).

Within the American mainstream, the history of women's cinema is as much a history of generic change as of social change. As many scholars have pointed out, Hollywood is a generic cinema, but its genres do not constitute a fixed repertoire. Genres by their nature shift and change, appear and disappear, and occur in unlikely cross-fertilised forms (see Neale 2000). As minor cinema, women's cinema operates through the major systems of genre, constrained by the possibilities at any given juncture, even as it works to extend these boundaries. In the studio era, the constraints of genre, along with the other constraints of the system, imposed real limitations on feminine and feminist expression in the movies. With the end of the studio era, filmmakers anticipated a release from these constraints, but in their absence, encountered new problems of expression and recognition in a commercial mass medium. Since the late 1980s, as Pam Cook notes, 'the increased gender fluidity and genre hybridity characteristic of the new Hollywood' has brought explicitly feminist themes to wider audiences (1998: 244–5), creating a new space for women's cinema in the mainstream. A new generation of directors has learned to negotiate generic constraints, playing reflexively on the limits they impose and self-consciously invoking their cultural history. However, although recent women's cinema has made great strides in the US mainstream, realistically it is fair to say that while it operates within generic paradigms, it can never match the confrontational rhetoric of the theorists of the 1970s. The next chapter examines some of the ways that this challenge has been met by experimental filmmakers.

2 PERFORMING AUTHORSHIP: SELF-INSCRIPTION IN WOMEN'S EXPERIMENTAL CINEMA

There is something extraordinary: the way the actress-auteurs are both on both sides of the camera, without this having any conse-quences. There is a calm violence which points up the difference with the male actor-auteur. Look at Lewis or Chaplin: for them, passing from one side of the camera to the other means risking travesty, feminization and playing with this risk. Nothing of the sort with women. (Daney 1977)

Women and the avant-garde

Many feminist critics have posited a special affinity between women filmmakers and experimental cinema. Annette Kuhn suggests that 'low investments of money and "professionalism" have meant that avant-garde cinema has historically been much more open than the film industry to women' (1982: 185) and Pam Cook (1981) notes a coincidence between the avant-garde's concern with personal self-expression and feminist interest in the private sphere, while Laura Mulvey proposes a strategic alliance between experimental film, post-structural theory and feminist politics based on 'a common interest in the politics of images and problems of aesthetic language' (1979: 7). But beyond these asser-tions of openness and affinity lies a complex and often problematic set of relationships. Women's involvement in the avant-garde of the early   twentieth century was limited by the social conventions of the time, while the meanings of femininity in avant-garde works are often startlingly misogynist, as in the case of Salvador Dali and Luis Buñuel's *Un Chien Andalou* (1929), which opens with an intentionally horrifying simulated assault on female vision. The post-war period brought only a limited improvement to this situation, despite the undisputed importance of a woman, Maya Deren, in establishing the ambitions and profile of the North American avant-garde.

Women's entry into avant-garde filmmaking may have been relatively unopposed, but, as B. Ruby Rich complains, female filmmakers are rarely elevated to the heights of the critical pantheon along with their male counterparts, and those who are may be subjected to 'Derenesque bury-the-mother maneuvers' (1998: 282). Rich is most scathing about the 1970s, the heyday of structural film: 'Imagine the seventies: a chosen circle of guys elevated as gods for their cutting-edge work, the deification of structuralism as the only way to make films, and a determinedly uncritical attitude towards representations of women on celluloid' (104). Patricia Mellencamp remarks that in the US avant-garde, although 'it was true that "woman" was not blatantly exchanged or commodified by avant-garde films, neither was she centrally figured. "She" seemed to vanish with very few traces, except as allied partisan, liberated lover or filmed mother/muse' (1990: 12). While Mulvey's argument for the affinity of feminism and avant-garde draws on the theorisation by Julia Kristeva and others of modernist writing as a privileged site of 'the feminine', Rich and Mellencamp seem more inclined to share Andreas Huyssen's understanding of modernism:

> It seems fairly obvious that the wholesale theorization of modernist writing as feminine simply ignores the powerful masculinist and misogynist current within the trajectory of modernism, a current which time and again openly states its contempt for women and for the masses. (1988: 49)

Whatever the extent of modern art's misogyny, it is certainly true that by the 1960s there had emerged a dominant version of the avant-garde project in which there could be very little place for gender as an issue. In an influential essay, Clement Greenberg argued that 'the unique and proper area of competence of each art coincided with all that was unique to the nature of its medium', a proposition readily embraced by adherents of 'pure film' and structural materialists (1965: 194). One of the major tasks confronting the feminist art, film and theory of the 1970s onwards was to widen the definition of work on 'the nature of the medium' to include work on the iconographic conventions which had fixed the meanings of femininity and the social relations in which culture is produced and consumed. Under the influence of the women's movement, an agenda very different from Greenberg's emerged, which prioritised the body, the personal and intersubjective power relations. Feminist art produced formal innovations out of the practical necessity of revising the 'one-dimensional gender inscriptions' (Huyssen 1988: 55) of both high and popular culture, rather than from a desire to join a predominantly male avant-garde.

Against this background, women's experimental cinema has developed with tactical allegiances to various avant-garde movements, but with a distinct set of concerns of its own which recur, with varied inflections due to cultural and institutional settings, in works with widely differing provenances. A number of these concerns are gathered up In the trope of authorial self-inscription which appears consistently in women's avant-garde films and which forms a distinctive aspect of their practice, although by no means its only defining feature. Strategies of self-inscription register the influences of avant-garde personal filmmaking, Godardian reflexivity, the autobiographical literature of the women's movement, the tradition of self-portraiture in women's painting, performance and body art, and the domestic associations of low-budget media (8mm film and video). Through authorial self-inscription, women filmmakers have been able to figure the terms of their engagement with the medium and its conventions, and, indeed, it is noticeable that many filmmakers (including Maya Deren, Chantal Akerman and Valie Export) move away from – or beyond – its most literal forms once they have established their style, and equally, that each generation of newcomers reinvents the trope for itself. The prominence of figurations of corporeality in this work gives some corroboration to Deleuze's suggestion that the importance of women directors comes from 'the way they have produced innovations in this cinema of bodies, as if women had to conquer the source of their own attitudes and the temporality which corresponds to them as individual or common gest' (1989: 196–7). Stripped of its essentialist assumptions, this is a useful formulation of one of the central problematics of women's experimental cinema: how to overcome the cultural coding of woman as 'an element of plot-space, a topos, a resistance, matrix and matter' (de Lauretis 1984: 119), to give agency to the body in the diegesis and embodiment to the author outside it.

Women and authorship

In her reconsideration of female authorship, Judith Mayne argues that for women 'the difficulty of saying "I"' (Mayne 1990: 92; the phrase comes from the German writer Christa Wolf) may be even greater in cinema than in writing. The cinema inherits all the 'patriarchal, phallic and proprietary implications' (97) of literary authorship, and in the evolution of its own conventions, adds a codification of audio-visuality structured by normative assumptions of masculinity and heterosexuality. Coded for 'to-be-looked-at-ness', in Mulvey's famous coinage, the woman is an object rather than a subject of vision, action and enunciation. Mayne puts it thus:

> The analysis of female authorship in the cinema raises somewhat different questions than does the analysis of male authorship, not only for the obvious reason that women have not had the same relationship to the institutions of cinema as men have, but also because the articulation of female authorship threatens to upset the erasure of "women" which is central to the articulation of "woman" in the cinema. (97)

In Film Studies, theorists have been concerned to complicate and deconstruct the notion of authorship; following Barthes, great emphasis has been placed on readers of texts and on the text as 'readerly', while theories of authorship have languished in a state of partial renovation since the 1970s. Yet for female filmmakers, for whom the act of authoring is already complicated by social conditions and cultural conventions, authorship is not so much a question of deconstruction as one of *recon*-struction. Insistence on the authoring presence of the woman outside the text is a formal and tactical necessity. To quote Mayne again, 'The notion of authorship is not simply a useful political strategy; it is crucial to the reinvention of cinema that has been undertaken by women filmmakers and feminist spectators' (97).

Within alternative cinema, women filmmakers have addressed 'the difficulty of saying "I"' by appearing in their own films, performing as themselves or others, using their voices on the soundtrack and working with autobiographical content. Hamid Naficy's (2001) argument about self-inscription in exilic cinema seems equally applicable to women's experimental cinema. Naficy suggests that the function of self-inscription in exilic cinema is to problematise both authorship and autobiography by structuring the films to suggest continuity but not identity between the author as an empirical person, outside the text, and the author as structure and system within the text. Thus, Naficy suggests 'filmmakers' relationship to their films and to the authoring agency within them is not solely one of parentage but also one of performance' (2001: 4). The performativity thus demonstrated cuts both ways of course: the mutual contamination of textual and extratextual identities underlines the constructedness of both. In its most sophisticated manifestations, the purpose of self-inscription is not the construction of a coherent subject position for the author, but the construction of a viable speaking position which, nonetheless, mirrors and enacts the author's experience of selfhood and embodiment as multiple and fragmented. In this chapter, I shall examine a number of examples of women filmmakers' practices of self-inscription, not only in order to show the prevalence of the trope and its association with female identity, but also as a way of tracing the history of women's experimental cinema as it cuts through a variety of contexts and practices.

The avant-garde author as movie star: Maya Deren

In the pre-history of feminist cinema, there is one particularly celebrated and influential model for female authorial self-inscription: Maya Deren's trilogy. Made in the 1940s, these three short films forecast the terms of women's subsequent engagement with alternative film, and intuitively anticipate many of the discoveries of feminist film theory. Maya Deren's critical reputation has shifted significantly in the four decades since her death in 1961. Originally canonised as the 'Mother of the American Underground Film', Deren was assigned a position of genealogical importance: she was seen as the missing link between two largely male traditions, the European avant-garde of the 1920s (in which Germaine Dulac, often described as the first feminist filmmaker, was a notable exception) and the American 'visionary' film of the 1950s and 1960s. Since the 1970s, critical re-evaluation has re-positioned her work as an important contribution to three distinct areas of debate: the status of film as an art form and its relationships with the other arts, the alternatives to Hollywood and its literary-theatrical aesthetic, and the necessity, for female authors and spectators, of redefining cinematic femininity (see Rabinovitz 1991). Deren addressed these issues through her films, in her theoretical writings, and in her energetic work building audiences for her films and those of others, and is, as a consequence, generally regarded as the single most important figure in the establishment of post-war avant-garde film culture in the US.

Without reducing Deren's films to a reflexive echo of her artistic career, one might argue that they are inlaid with an image of the paradoxes of female cinematic authorship, heightened by her deliberate cultivation of a flamboyantly exotic femininity. Deren's concern with identity is one of the most striking aspects of her life and work: in her short life, she adopted many identities, through two nationalities, three marriages and three or four careers. Of the six films she completed, three offer classic instances of avant-garde self-inscription: *Meshes of the Afternoon* (1943), *At Land* (1944) and *Ritual in Transfigured Time* (1946). The prevalence of filmmaker-actors in the US avant-garde has been noted by P. Adams Sitney, who suggests that it is accounted for not only by economy,

practicality, and an autobiographical impulse, but also by a new understanding of the propensities of film as a medium:

> There is also another, more subtle reason which accounts for the
> number of self-acted films, particularly at the beginning of the
> avant-garde film movement in America: film becomes a process
> of self-realization. Many film-makers seem to have been unable to
> project the highly personal psychological drama that these films
> reveal into other characters' minds. They were realizing the themes
> of their films through making and acting them. These were true
> psycho-dramas. (1979: 18)

Though the term 'psycho-drama' belies Deren's formalism, the notion
of 'self-realization' seems appropriate given the extent to which Deren's
identity as an artist was achieved through her films. Long before Andy
Warhol created his underground stars, Deren understood how the
circulation of her image might boost her artistic career. From the name
Maya, Hindi for 'illusion' (Rabinovitz 1991: 50), which she changed from
Eleonora shortly before she became a filmmaker, through the bohemian
clothes she made for herself, to the famous still from *Meshes of the Afternoon* which she used in publicity, Deren developed her own 'star image':

> Deren became the best-known representative of the postwar
> independent cinema discourse, perhaps, because she herself
> was the object of attention as often as her films and ideas. Her
> bodily appearance is important not because she was a woman but
> because it was the site for Deren's 'star' construction as a film-
> maker marked by contradictory desires for power and the pursuit of
> a feminine image within discourse. (Rabinovitz 1991: 49)

The ambivalence of Deren's relationship with her star image is thema-
tised in the trilogy in tropes of splitting and doubling and inscribed
more subtly as a tension between her role as a performer within the film
and her authorial, poetic aspirations. She was noted for her amateur
dancing, and her interest and participation in voodoo rituals, as well

as being involved with dance professionally in her youth, as secretary
to the choreographer Katherine Dunham. Her interest in dance supplies
much of the originality of her work: she pioneered the use of cinematic
processes such as slow motion and freeze frame to create dance movements from everyday gestures, and her editing style, using cuts on
movement to connect gestures, has been compared to dance (Sitney
1979: 24). On the other hand, her long-standing interest in poetry (she
wrote her MA thesis on Symbolist and Imagist poetry), and her understanding of her own films as poetic structures (see Deren *et al.* 1963)
suggest that she also thought of film in linguistic terms. In a letter to
James Card, she compares her entry into filmmaking to 'coming home
into a world whose vocabulary, syntax, grammar was my mother-tongue',
and *Meshes* to 'the first speech of a mute' (Deren 1965: 29), a particularly
interesting comparison for her to make in view of the absence of spoken
language from her films (the reason for this is entirely practical: until
the early 1960s, suitable, inexpensive equipment was not available for
filmmakers to make synchronised soundtracks for 16mm films; even the
music on most prints of *Meshes* was added much later by Deren's third
husband, Teiji Ito). That silence should be a condition of self-expression in the medium in which Deren sought to establish a voice perhaps
explains the intensity of the dialectic of entrapment and escape in her
work. The transmutation of a desire for verbal self-expression into movement and gesture evokes the metonymic displacements of melodrama in
which the burden of repressed communication is borne by the body and
its mise-en-scène, with the crucial difference that, in the absence of the
constraints of verisimilitude, excess emerges not as embarrassment but
as psychic heroics.

Deren's first film, *Meshes of the Afternoon*, co-authored with cinematographer Alexander Hammid just after their marriage, is a cautionary
tale of feminine enunciation in a masculine idiom. The film was categorised for many years as surrealist, but more recent critical evaluations
have noted its oppositional incorporation of Hollywood iconography:

> *Meshes* seems less related to European surrealism than to the
> Freudian flashbacks and sinister living-rooms that typify Hollywood's

wartime 'noir' films. Located in some hilly L.A. suburb, the house where Deren's erotic, violent fantasy was filmed might be around the corner from Barbara Stanwyck's place in *Double Indemnity*.[1]

The spiral narrative structure of the film follows the same pattern of events five times in all: a woman enters a house, sits down and falls asleep, and has three variants on the same dream, in which she pursues a hooded figure with a mirrored face into the house, where mundane objects move by themselves or transform into other objects and space becomes unstable. Each version of the dream doubles the protagonist, until there are four Derens, including the dreamer. Just as the third, most malevolent double is about to stab the original Deren with a large knife, she is replaced by a man, played by Hammid, who bends down to wake her with a kiss. The couple go upstairs where she lies on the bed and he caresses her; she responds by attacking him with the knife. At the moment of impact, his face is replaced by a mirror, which shatters into pieces that fall into the sea. In the final narrative loop, the man retraces the woman's steps, only to find her dead in her armchair, festooned with seaweed and shards of mirror.

Although it is tempting to read the opening and closing sequences as a diegetic reality enclosing three dream sequences, the inclusion of magical events in both situates the film more ambiguously in a fictional universe where fantasy and reality permeate each other. The film's oneiric systems and its prominent use of classic Freudian symbols (a knife, a key, a purse and a flower) invite a psychoanalytic reading in which the splitting of identity results from a resistance to culturally correct femininity, although Deren – whose father was a psychiatrist – rejected such symptomatic approaches. In her own notes, Deren claimed that the primary concern of the film was 'the use of the cinematic technique in such a way as to create a world: to put on film the feeling which a human being experiences about an incident, rather than to accurately record the incident' (Deren 1965: 1). The cinematic techniques which Hammid deploys so skilfully in *Meshes* are, for an avant-garde film, surprisingly conventional: the eyeline matches and matches on action are Hollywood staples and even the double exposure was regularly used in Hollywood twin movies, such as *Dark Mirror* (R. Siodmak, 1946). What is unusual about the film is the particular subjective vision served by these techniques, a woman's vision, and the volatility which this vision imparts to the world it encounters. Re-read through the filter of contemporary feminism, the project of *Meshes* is the reworking of conventional cinematic looking relations for an active female subject.

The subjective camerawork of the first sequence opens the film with a clear statement of its interest in the woman's point of view. However, the longer the image of the protagonist's face is withheld, the more mystery accrues to her, resulting in her coding as hero *and* enigma. When subjective camerawork gives way to a more conventional shot/reverse shot rhetoric after the end of the opening sequence, this double positioning is maintained: the woman appears at both poles of the alternation, as if her appropriation of the look has failed to release her from her function as its object. Instead, her look generates multiple versions of herself, variously coded for specular pathology (one is made up like a film noir femme fatale; another wears spectacles with mirrored baubles in place of lenses). At the same time, the animation of the home and the objects within it evokes the mischief of the sorcerer's apprentice: in a world in which the woman controls the look, any object might be instilled with agency.

When looking relations finally short-circuit in the murder/suicide scene, the man is introduced and appears momentarily to stabilise things, assuming the power of the look and repositioning the woman as its object. The protagonist's violent response momentarily breaks the frame, evoking an alternative diegesis in which the mirror of specularity is swallowed by the sea, a well-worn icon of femininity. The film's final sequence is almost a coda, and is open to a number of interpretations, of which the most obvious is that the protagonist chooses death rather than submission to representational conventions which assume her objectification. *Meshes* predates the women's movement by 25 years, but if anything, this renders its confrontation of patriarchal film conventions all the more interesting, since it arises from lived necessity rather than the insights of theory.

At Land emerges very directly from the concerns and techniques of *Meshes*, but abandons the earlier film's confrontation of Hollywood in favour of a feminine fantasy of initiation and flight. Formally, the film is built entirely around the technique of false continuity created by the match on action and the eyeline match. The protagonist, Deren again, inhabits a purely cinematic landscape in which she clambers from the beach, to the bushes, to a banquet table, and embarks on a series of encounters that seem concerned with sociality, sexuality and power, before returning to the sea. Its structure is more linear than that of *Meshes*, and despite its oneiric imagery, there are no direct depictions or evocations of the dream state in the later film; the protagonist appears more like a lucid dreamer, controlling her own experience. The film's point of view system is more streamlined, as Sitney notes: 'The rich texture of interlocking alternations of subjective camera and synecdochic framing of elaborate and dramatic pans, which *Meshes* owed to the creative involvement of Hammid, disappears here, as the photographer [Hella Heyman] worked under the direction of the author-actress' (1979: 23).

This denigration of the later film overlooks a significant stylistic development: the binarism of subject and object in *Meshes* is deterministic, creating a point of view system predicated on unequal heterosexual relations and therefore prophetic of the protagonist's ultimate collision with the male gaze; the simpler, more 'objective' system of *At Land* avoids both the involuted interiority of *Meshes* and its profound entanglement in heterosexual looking relations. In view of these systemic differences, it is interesting to compare the circumstances under which doubles appear in the two films. In *Meshes*, the first of the doubles appears in a dream, summoned up from the woman's unconscious. Subsequent doubles make their first appearances in the field of vision of their predecessor, provoked by her aberrant, active look. In *At Land*, the woman encounters a series of earlier selves, or herself at a series of earlier moments, on her flight back to the sea; they glance at her, in surprise, but she pays them no attention. Stripped of its psychological significance, doubling figures as an exfoliation of the personality, a shedding of skins that recalls Virginia Woolf's 'selves of which we are built up, one on top of another, as plates are piled on a waiter's hand' (1967: 217–18). If *Meshes* is a cautionary tale, *At Land* is a fantasy of survival in which the female protagonist literally surpasses herself.

The third film in the series, *Ritual in Transfigured Time*, is a rite of passage film in which a widow is transformed into a bride, although she flees the groom and marries the sea. Anticipating the 'happenings' of the 1960s, the first half of the film reworks footage of a party with such starry guests as Gore Vidal and Anaïs Nin into an elaborate collective ritual. The second half continues the experiments with filming dance which Deren began in *A Study in Choreography for the Camera* (1945), and centres on a dance of courtship, from which the widow escapes into the sea. Deren uses a variety of processes to create a specifically cinematic ritual: the party and the subsequent dance are rendered ritualistic by the use of slow motion, repetition and freeze frame and the final sequence in the sea uses negative photographic processing to turn a black figure into a white one.

The film marks a turning point in Deren's career, a shift in her interest from the personal to the collective which would eventually lead her to anthropology. Several of her writings on ritual suggest that one of its attractions for her was the minimisation of personal identity ('A ritual is characterised by the de-personalization of the individual' (Deren 1965: 10)), and it seems conceivable that she had begun to perceive the identity she had created for herself as in some ways burdensome. Certainly the manner of her self-inscription in *Ritual,* the last film in which she appears, suggests that this was so. In a further permutation of the formal realisation and meaning of doubling, the central role of a widow who is transformed into a bride is shared between Deren and the dancer Rita Christiani. The timing and nature of Deren's appearances are suggestive: she appears first, and plays a short scene with Christiani, who takes up some yarn which Deren is unwinding from a skein. Deren disappears once Christiani has wound all the yarn into a ball, to reappear only for brief moments, spliced into the film's continuity, in the final flight sequence.

In *Ritual*, doubling operates as surrogation, enabling Deren to begin to move towards the usual position of the author as enunciator, delegating story-telling to the fictional characters (in a nice literalism, Christiani takes up the narrative thread). The trance-like demeanour of Christiani and the other performers relates this surrogation to possession. At the same time, the cultural milieu invoked by the party sequence places Deren as an artist amongst others, just as the film's invocation of other art forms stakes a claim for cinema in the art world, as Rabinovitz notes: '*Ritual* did not so much rewrite a woman's cinema but rather situated an alternative base within the vanguard arts from which one could sound a woman's voice' (1991: 71). In the last film of the trilogy, Deren escapes from the hall of mirrors she created with Hammid, into the impersonality of ritual and art. Deren's legacy for women's cinema emerges in the direct influence she had on the work of later filmmakers such as Storm de Hirsch, Barbara Hammer, Su Friedrich and Sally Potter, but also indirectly, in the convergence of film with the art world. After the arid 1950s, the conjunction of art, film and performance proved fruitful again in the 1960s, when self-inscription became a frontline strategy in the feminist initiative to reclaim the female body.

Body language: Carolee Schneemann, Valie Export and Mara Mattuschka

Carolee Schneemann trained as a painter in the late 1950s, and immediately conceived an interest in her own body. She recalls that her interest in self-portraiture was dismissed as narcissism by her professor, and comments dryly that 'the male students doing their endless self-portrait studies were not considered "narcissistic". But then they did leave out their bodies!' (Schneemann 1997: 193). In works such as *Eye Body* (1963), Schneemann broke down the boundaries between painting and performance. Yves Klein's human paintbrush had established that the nude could be the painter's instrument as well as his model; Schneemann extended this use of the body in two directions: the body became part of the painting-construction and at the same time, authored the work: 'Covered in paint, grease, chalk, ropes, plastic, I establish my body as visual territory. Not only am I an image maker, but I explore the image values of flesh as material I choose to work with' (52). Along with other performance artists associated with the Fluxus movement and Actionism, Schneemann reinterpreted the nude; uniquely, she aimed not to demystify or defile the nude, but to subjectify it and animate it with a primal feminine energy: 'The nude was being used in early Happenings as an object (often an "active" object), I was using the nude as myself – the artist – and as a primal, archaic force which could unify energies I discovered as visual information' (52). Her autobiographical short film *Fuses* (1967) (part of a trilogy, including *Plumb Line* (1971) and *Kitch's Last Meal* (1973–8)),[2] extends this work, and was, in fact begun in response to her experience of appearing in Stan Brakhage's films *Loving* (1957) and *Cat's Cradle* (1959). *Fuses* depicts Schneemann's love-making with her partner of the time, James Tenney. Filming was undertaken by both of the participants, and the footage was treated to various processes and edited by Schneemann:

> There were whole sections where the film is chopped up and laid onto either black or transparent leader and taped down. I also put some of the film into the oven to bake it; I soaked it in all sorts of acids and dyes to see what would happen. I cut out details of imagery and repeated them. I worked on the film for three years. (Schneemann in Youngblood 1970: 119)

The result is doubly autobiographical: intensely intimate, in its close-up portrayal of bodies and sexual acts, and densely textured, marked by its artisanal, domestic production, with a non-linear organisation that mimics a participant perception or memory of events, rather than objectifying those events. The filmic vocabulary of *Fuses* parallels that of pornography, but its texture and organisation sharply differentiates it: the scratched, painted and baked celluloid draws attention to the film as process and surface, in tension with its graphic depictions of fellatio, cunnilingus and masturbation, making it at once explicit and obscure, while the fragmentary and rhythmic editing patterns and the inclusion of quotidian details – Schneemann running on the beach, Tenney driving his car, Schneemann's cat, Kitch, pottering about – suffuse the film with a lyrical banality, a poetry of the everyday. Instead of a narrative, Schneemann's editing creates a field of polymorphous pleasures that are as aesthetic as they are erotic. Lacking sustained point-of-view systems, alternating between shots attributable to Schneemann's point of view, Tenney's points of view and even the cat's, the film is an experiment in intersubjectivity – one of the meanings of its title.[3]

Fuses has been described as 'historically anomalous' (James 1989: 317), which is an understatement of the notoriety conferred on it by its lack of synchronicity with prevailing fashions in the worlds of art, film and feminism in which it made its impact. Emerging at a difficult moment, the end of the libertarian 1960s and the beginning of the puritanical 1970s, the film was equally unpopular with the 'black and white aquarian stalin- ists' of 1968 (Heathcote Williams quoted in Schneemann 1997: 278), the 'avant-garde boys' club' and the feminist 'sex cops' (Rich 1998: 21–2). Schneemann's utopian advocacy of female heterosexual pleasure post- dated interest in the writings of Wilhelm Reich and pre-dated the rein- terpretations of female sexuality promulgated by Luce Irigaray and other French theorists, while she was twenty years ahead of queer cinema in her positive appropriation of sexual iconography. Her interest in goddess cults and feminine creativity met with embarrassment in the heyday of a feminist materialism which regarded femininity in all its guises as a patriarchal social construction.

The outrage which greeted public screenings of *Fuses* in the 1970s was so great that Schneemann took to crawling out of theatres during the show under cover of darkness (Rich 1998: 21). As James puts it: 'The possible effect on contemporary film of Schneemann's love in the medium was defused and diffused by the terror her vision evoked. The film could hardly be seen, either by the avant-garde establishment or by the women's movement' (James 1989: 321). Schneemann perceives a continuity in these diverse reactions to her work, a resistance to work in which the female artist crosses the line between authorship and performance:

The question that I asked [in *Eye Body*] was: 'Could I be both an image in it and the image maker? Could I have authority there?' The answer at that time was 'Absolutely not!' It has to do with some conflict still present: why no work of mine is in any museum in America and I have a huge body of work. (quoted in Harper 1998: 192)

Schneemann recounts that after 18 years without a dealer, one finally agreed to represent her as a painter, on the proviso that, to avoid confusing the market, she agree not to perform in New York for the next 4 years.

Many of Schneemann's concerns are shared by her Austrian contemporary, Valie Export, although Export's frame of reference is closer to 1970s and 1980s feminist theory and current technofeminism. *Fuses* aspires to the condition of painting: its reclamation of femininity is accomplished on the basis of the romantic assumption of the authority of the artist and the authenticity of the body. Export's work, on the contrary, envisions the female body as a continually shifting cultural and historical matrix. By juxtaposing different media in 'medial anagrams', as she describes her works (Mueller 1994: 213), Export shows how constructions of the female body depend on social and technological conditions of representation. Her method is not to attack representation, but to make 'ontological leaps'[4] between different systems of representation, foregrounding the expressive limitations and prescriptive conventions of each, 'to force the body's code out of the frozen history of culture' (Export in Mueller 1994: 114). Her view of the body is succinctly summed up by Roswitha Mueller: 'The body embedded in and part of a system of communication is neither identical with this system nor immune to it' (xx). Like Schneemann, Export explores the cultural contradictions opened up by the presentation of the female author's body as source, form and content of the artwork, but unlike Schneemann, she depicts the body as part of a continuous semiotic exchange with the world it inhabits:

> From the beginning, the body in Export's work was conceived as the bearer of signs, signals and information. This designation goes in two directions. On one hand, it means that the body is the site of cultural determinations, the place where the law of society is engraved onto the individual. On the other, it also implies the body's capacity to signal to the outside world and communicate with it. (Mueller 1994: 31)

In her early expanded cinema works, Export used her own body as the instrument of a critique of the cinematic apparatus. In *Tap and Touch*

Cinema (*Tapp und Tastkino*, 1968), she constructed a small movie theatre from a box which she wore on her naked upper body; in the street, passers-by were invited to reach beyond the little theatre's curtain and feel her breasts, thus reversing cinema's voyeuristic substitution of looking for touching, and bringing the spectator's involvement out into the open. In *Genital Panic* (*Genitalpanik*, 1969) she walked through the audience in a porno cinema wearing jeans with the crotch cut out, confronting the spectators with the reality axiomatically disavowed by the mechanisms of fetishism. An important component of these works, for Export, was the woman's ability to control her own sexual availability, and, although by current feminist standards, the work's transformation of woman from object to subject of pleasure seems less than complete (Mueller 1994: 18), this was its aim, and also the central tenet of the Feminist Actionism which Export proclaimed:

Just as action aims at achieving the unity of actor and material, perception and action, subject and object, Feminist Actionism seeks to transform the object of male natural history, the material 'woman', subjugated and enslaved by the male creator, into an independent actor and creator, object of her own history. For without the ability to express oneself and without a field of action, there can be no human dignity. (Export in Mueller 1994: 29)

Through her practice of Feminist Actionism, Export transformed the unthinking misogyny of her male peers, the Viennese Actionists, whose use of the female body reflected the sexual politics of the time: 'Women's bodies were primarily passive objects to be acted upon rather than actors in their own right. The packaged, smeared, used and abused bodies of women were central to some Actionist fantasies of destruction' (Mueller 1994: xix). Her aim, however, was not simply to refigure the female body as subject rather than object, author instead of model, but to demonstrate the incompleteness of these distinctions. Another expanded cinema work, *Adjoined Dislocations* (*Adjungierte Dislokationen*, 1973), explores the relationship between film and the body by creating a film-body or body-film. Using her own body as a sort of tripod, Export strapped two

73

8mm cameras to her chest and back and filmed her surroundings, while being filmed by a 16mm camera. The resulting three-screen projection prosthetically conjoins the body and technology in an early prefiguration of the feminist cyborg. Roswitha Mueller describes the body in Export's work as an 'expanded body', although it is also the inverse of this, in Export's phrase, an 'environmental body'.

More extended meditation on the idea of social technologies takes place in Export's fiction features, particularly the first of these, *Invisible Adversaries* (*Unsichtbare Gegner,* 1977), which has been described as a feminist *Invasion of the Bodysnatchers*. The film concerns a Viennese artist, Anna, whose observation of the aggressiveness that surrounds her leads her to believe that humanity is being taken over by an alien force, the Hyksos. The invaders appear as doppelgangers, briefly depicted for the spectator when Anna's mirror image performs independent actions, and in photographs showing the doubled image of the psychiatrist who diagnoses her as a paranoid schizophrenic. In the tradition of the fantastic, the film pivots between case study and science fiction, refusing to direct the spectator to an unambiguous conclusion about Anna's sanity. The *unheimlich* world which Anna inhabits is created by the assemblage of fragments including rudimentary narrative, pixilated and montaged sequences which animate objects and objectify people, dream sequences, found footage and pre-existing artworks by Export. In each of these registers, social and representational conventions are made strange: food comes to life on Anna's chopping board, a witty parallel montage compares her ablutions to the preparation of her boyfriend's dinner, Export's video *Silent Language* (*Stille Sprache*) morphs Renaissance madonnas into modern women in the idiom of twentieth-century advertising posing awkwardly with household appliances, Anna makes herself a moustache from her pubic hair, a photograph of a vagina grunts loudly as it is being developed... But despite its Viennese origin and its Freudian puns, *Invisible Adversaries* posits doubling and splitting not as classical Freudian mechanisms, but as the manifestation of an alienation from physicality induced by representation (or mechanical reproduction, in Benjamin's apt phrase). Valerie Manenti has suggested that although the body as origin and site of female identity appears to be the central question in Export's work, in fact, her 'notion of "body language" (*körpersprache*) poses an ironic relation to these questions that actually acknowledges "the end of the body" or at least the final break with the way in which we understand it to be a biological, existential, or meta-physical entity' (Manenti n.d.). Manenti proposes that in Export's short film *Syntagma* (1983), 'body speech' is not enunciated from a point of cohesion, but is distributed throughout the text, like machine language in computer circuitry; a proposal that also makes sense of the use of doubling, schizophrenia, animism of objects and collaging of other texts in her feature films:

> Export seems critical of the opposition between a metaphysics of the body, nostalgically and ceremonially retained in our age, and the body of the 21st century which is functionally the equivalent of a machine that produces meaning. As the speaker (enunciator) of the film she seems in between the opposition – at the wake of the organic body preceding the creation of the completely intelligible body. (Manenti n.d.)

This transitional positioning accounts for the pervasiveness of dialogues between humanism and anti-humanism in this film and Export's third feature, *The Practice of Love* (*Die Praxis der Liebe*, 1984). In both films, the protagonists recoil from the dehumanising effects of capitalism's social technologies, and in both, they use technologies of representation as tools to investigate and resist this dehumanisation. In *Invisible Adversaries,* Anna works on a video piece in which women – including the filmmaker Helke Sander – are asked to respond to the question 'When is a human being a woman?' The implied reverse-form of the question, 'When is a woman a human being?' draws together the film's thematics, its play with the animate and inanimate, its exploration of the body's double structure as matter and mind, self and other. When Anna's boyfriend Peter responds to her demands for intimacy and empathy with the remark that 'human beings are merely side-effects of overlapping systems', the film pinpoints the problem, for feminism, of anti-humanism, especially that variant which has more to do with masculinist expediency than marxist philosophy: the incommensurate effects of the theoretical renunciation of subjectivity for men, who may take it for granted, and women, to whom it represents a hard-won achievement.

Export inscribes herself into the film at several levels: she actually appears, in some of the incorporated works, and at the same time the character Anna stands in for her, sharing her profession and her then boyfriend, the artist Peter Weibel, who wrote the lines he performs in the film. As author-in-the-text, she also is doubly inscribed, as the maker of the incorporated artworks and as the author of the film. Her multiple self-inscription constitutes a simultaneous insistence on and dispersal of her subjectivity which erodes the qualitative distinction between extradiegetic and intradiegetic authorship; moreover, her method, which, as Mueller notes, is not so much narration as bricolage (1994: 126), allows her to deal with her own authoring body as an object amongst others, caught up in the text's circuits along with actors, buildings, props, animals, vehicles, photographs, found footage and all the other 'ready-mades' which inhabit the film. Gary Indiana's (2000) description of Export's aesthetic as 'culinary', captures the pleasure in materiality of her work, although it might be more accurate to situate it somewhere between cookery and code, a bricolage of objects and signs which erodes the distinction between the two orders, insisting on the power of each to transform the other.

The fundamental optimism in Export's work springs from her belief in the capacity of human beings to resist reification. An altogether darker – although comic – version of body language can be seen in several short films made in the 1980s by Export's compatriot, Mara Mattuschka. *Kugelkopf* (*Ballhead*, 1985) is a six-minute pun on the German word for a golf-ball style typewriter printhead. The film centres on a shocking and funny performance which has been seen as a riposte to the eye-slashing in *Un Chien Andalou*: Mattuschka, in the persona of her alter ego Mimi Minus, shaves her head with a razor blade, cutting her scalp in the process, then wraps it in muslin on which she daubs letters with black paint. Finally – at which point the spectator gets the joke – she begins to 'print' by smashing her head against a glass screen placed in front of the camera, covering it with thick black lettering. In the film's high-contrast black and white images, blood and paint are indistinguishable, and by the film's end Mimi Minus/Mattuschka and the screen are a sticky mess of both. In *Kaiserschnitt* (*Caesarean Section*, 1987), Mimi Minus is cut open and gives birth to the alphabet, in the form of alphabet soup (nursery food, significantly), which she then arranges in correct order using tweezers.

Mattuschka's work, like Export's, has often been contextualised in terms of Viennese Actionism, although its degraded physicality and internalised violence might equally be read as punk aesthetics. As in Export's work, the notion that the body inhabits sign systems is literalised in the playful collapse of abstract signification into concrete physicality, with the crucial difference that instead of attempting to create new body-sign relationships, Mattuschka offers comically regressive fantasies of a language that is decidedly not phallogocentric, with the head-shaving ritual standing in for symbolic castration, and language itself originating in the womb. In one critic's assessment, 'Mara Mattuschka wants to get to the things themselves, she wants to reverse the constitutive insufficiency of language, in order, via pleasure in art, to find pleasure in the body and thence pleasure in being' (Tscherkassky 1994). Thus the trajectory that begins with Schneemann comes almost full circle: the body, which the first generation of feminist film artists struggled to release from mute objectification, reclaims language for a messy materiality.

Adventures of the voice: Akerman and Rainer

The works discussed above may be situated within a cinema of corporeality. Several films by two of the most prominent experimental filmmakers in women's cinema, Yvonne Rainer and Chantal Akerman, have explored an alternative conception of female authorship as an 'adventure of the voice' (Daney 1977),[5] the aptness of which is striking in view of the fact that most of the terms for thinking about authorship in film theory metaphorise filmmaking as speech, while remaining obscure on the issue of its source. The concept of enunciation treats cinematic authorship as a speech act, but a speech act without a speaker, just as cinematic narration lacks a narrator (Stam *et al.* 1992: 62). In general, this absence guarantees the reliability and authority of the narration or enunciation; where narration is embedded within the film, in the form of diegetic characters whose voices are heard in synchronous sound, enunciative authority is diminished.

Of extradiegetic voice-over narration, Kaja Silverman notes that despite its rarity in fiction film, 'the disembodied voice can be seen as "exemplary" for male subjectivity, attesting to an achieved invisibility, omniscience and discursive power'; conversely, to disembody the female voice in fiction film is to 'challenge every conception by means of which we have previously known woman within Hollywood film, since it is precisely as *body* that she is constructed there' (1988: 164). This accounts for the prevalence, in women's experimental cinema, of films which play against the conventions of synchronised sound to create separations and disjunctions of body and voice. In these works: 'the female voice is often shown to coexist with the female body only at the price of its own impoverishment and entrapment. Not surprisingly, therefore, it generally pulls away from any fixed locus within the image track, away from the constraints of synchronization' (141). The rearticulation of voice and body also has historical and economic dimensions: the development of synchronous sound in the late 1920s constituted only one of film technology's possible evolutionary trajectories, and one which the avant-garde has consistently challenged, on ideological grounds and from necessity, as a result of the difficulty and expense of synchronising sound.

The notion of a personal voice is a useful starting point for a consideration of the films of Chantal Akerman. A number of Akerman's films deal directly with autobiographical material, and others do so indirectly; in several, she plays a character who resembles herself. However, her deployment of autobiographical reference is diffracted and displaced so that, as Janet Bergstrom says, it 'serves a complex function, one which draws on a woman's lived experience while at the same time complicating the question "who speaks" by dispersing the origin of the enunciation across many positions' (Penley & Bergstrom 1985: 299).

In *Je, tu, il, elle* (*I, You, He, She,* 1974) Akerman uses linguistic and formal play as a pretext for an exploration of the relationships between self and other, as well as those between self and self. The film is a minimalist fiction in three parts, in which a protagonist, played by Akerman, sequesters herself in a room for several weeks where she tries to write a letter and eats caster sugar from a bag, then hitches a lift with a truck-driver and gives him a hand-job, and finally visits a woman, a former or current lover, with whom she has sex. Akerman compounds the ambiguities generated by her performance in the film by giving the protagonist no name, and naming the performer in the final credits simply as 'Julie', despite the inclusion of the family names of the other actors. In effect, Akerman inscribes herself in the film three times, as Chantal Akerman the author, as the young female protagonist, and as Julie the actor. The relationships between these 'selves' and the other characters undergo a series of permutations in the course of the film, which relate to, but do not actually match, the series of pronouns in the title, shown neatly chalked on a blackboard at the film's opening.

Most analyses of the film begin from the notion that 'je' might refer to the protagonist, 'il' to the truck-driver, and 'elle' to the woman lover, but the 'tu' is more ambiguous, possibly referring to the addressee of the letter or to the mode of address which 'je' establishes with 'il' and 'elle' in turn. The 'tu' is verbalised, on the soundtrack, but not definitively assigned a body, and this is mirrored by a splitting of the 'je' between sound and Image In the first segment: instead of sync sound, the image of the protagonist is combined with a first person voice-over that gives unreliable descriptions of the on-screen activities, marked by temporal mismatches, actions described before or after they are shown, and unverifiable information – 'I painted the furniture blue', when the protagonist is not seen painting, and no colour change is registered in the black and white film. Indeed the film begins with one such disjuncture, when the voice-over announces 'And I left', an action which is not performed until the end of the film. This divergence opens a gap between voice and body which rules out autobiographical identity as a simple rationale for the co-existence of author, character and performer. The organisation of the film and the counterpointing of sound and image serve to maximise the lack of fixity inherent in the title's pronominal shifters – linguistic forms whose meaning depends absolutely on who speaks them (as in the child's verbal game: 'I'm me', 'no, you're you'). Maureen Turim reads this lack of fixity as an indecidability at the heart of the text: 'It is as if the author in writing her story could not decide on the voice of narration. So she films. So she performs. Or, to be more precise, she offers artificial enunciations in the filmic performative' (1999: 14).

In the second and third parts of the film, the disjunctive use of sound recedes, to be replaced by other means of creating pronominal indecidability, as, for instance, when the truck-driver looks directly at the camera, which is positioned to represent Akerman's point of view during the only moment at which she is off-screen, during the hand-job (the only diegetic event to be created cinematically rather than performed for the camera). Mayne reads this moment as a brief fusion of Akerman's two roles as performer and filmmaker (1990: 130), although it might equally mark a retreat by Akerman from the position of performer to that of author. The staging and framing of the protagonist's encounters spatialises the theme of subject/object relations in such a way as to imply a systematic exploration of ways of representing intersubjective connections, whilst questioning the terms of their representability and even possibility. Thus the failed letter-writing functions as a prelude to the missed communications which follow. In the second part, the protagonist makes little effort to assimilate herself to the truck-driver's milieu, and in her repeated positioning at the edge of the frame appears in every way liminal. At the same time, language, which could facilitate the connection and which, uniquely in the film, holds this section together, is mocked when the truck-driver's speech exceeds its erotic and narrative purposes – his description of the off-screen masturbation, which articulates his preferences and his pleasure, but also supplies a lack in the on-screen representation – and lapses into narrative redundancy with the description of an on-screen event of no erotic consequence ('I'm putting my head on the wheel'). In the final part, the crux of much critical debate around the film, a monosyllabic verbal exchange mostly about food precedes an awkward and silent sexual encounter, after which the protagonist departs.

Considering the question of whether the organisation of the film should be read as a progression, from isolation, via heterosexuality to lesbian fulfilment,[6] and, indeed, whether it is a lesbian film, Mayne concludes negatively, but asserts nevertheless that *Je, tu, il, elle* 'attempts nothing less than the rewriting of the cinematic scenario that prescribes formulaic relations between those terms along the lines of heterosexual symmetry' (134). In a similar vein, Turim suggests that the film both fulfils and escapes psychoanalytic interpretation, offering an alternative way through a 'gap in identity' (1999: 21) to explore newer possibilities than the already-known identities that populate psychoanalysis. Ivone Margulies suggests that 'liminality is posited not as the ground for a future, delineated, identity but as an image of a mutant, transient one' (1996: 111). Several critics quote Narboni's description of the film as: 'Discourse in the fourth person singular, which is neither the histrionics of subjectivity (the "I"), nor the despotic quality of interpellation and demand (the "you"), nor the objectifying horror of the non-person (the "he/she")' (cited in Turim 1999: 10). Identity in *Je, tu, il, elle* is rendered at once self-evident, in the simplicity and exhaustive duration of the film's images, questionable, as a result of its mismatched narrative grammar, and absurd, in the obtuse eccentricity of Akerman's performance.

News From Home (1976) is an epistolary film which deals with subjectivity and displacement. Long takes of nondescript New York streets, subways and sidewalks are combined with a soundtrack of ambient noise and intermittent readings of English translations of letters written to Akerman by her mother during her first visit to the city in 1972. There is no on-screen protagonist, only the steady, estranged gaze of the camera. The letters, which are repetitive, tender, querulous and mundane, are read in a heavily-accented monotone which is sometimes drowned out by traffic sounds. An exilic structure of feeling is created by the transmutation of alienation, absence and distance into formal principles: the film maintains a rigorous separation between the personal off-screen space which anchors point of view and voice, and the public space on-screen, which is observed with detached curiosity. The majority of the shots are static, many of them centring the street so that its lines of perspective dominate as they recede towards a vanishing point, giving depth and direction to the image. Travelling shots predominate in the last portion of the film, as it proceeds to its final shot, an extreme long shot, taken from a ferry, of Manhattan receding in the distance. The famous skyline (dominated by the twin towers of the World Trade Center) is the film's first conventional image of New York, and for many viewers may be the first indication of its location. This progression, from mostly static fragments to mobility and a recognisable 'big picture', taken in conjunction with the film's themes of separation and individuation from the mother, tempts one to read into it a linear, diachronic evolution, as if the film were recapitulating the infant's entry into culture in terms of the elaboration of a 'film language' of movement, cognition and articulation (in this reading, the film's emphasis on the mother rather than the father takes on particular significance, positing the utopian possibility of access to a symbolic which is not determined by the paternal signifier).

However, such an evolutionary reading is undercut by the synchronic organisation of subjects (you and I), temporalities (then and now) and locations (here and there) in a pattern of separation and conjunction which may suggest psychological blockage or, alternately, might be understood as a refusal of the Oedipal dramatisation of separation from the mother. The film's system resolutely denies intersubjective contact: the letters receive no replies and interaction between the camera and those it films is limited to people's avoidance or return of the camera's look. Against this, Akerman poses the mother-daughter relationship as fusion: the daughter's voicing of the letters ventriloquises the mother in a performance which expresses both, in the words of one and the ambivalent feelings of the other. As Margulies notes, this is another instance of Akerman's use of shifters to undercut the notion of individual identity: 'the voice issues from and is directed at the same place; it echoes from a paradoxical space, both source and end, short-circuiting communication' (1996: 151). The absence of corporeality in the film, the fact that neither mother, nor daughter, is present as an image functions as a break with the iconography of the feminine which would inscribe them as objects rather than subjects, and at the same time, allows Akerman to develop an understanding of subjectivity as relational rather than individual.

In Akerman's films, language and speech function as faultlines, revealing the mutability or heterogeneity within an apparently unified identity; in Rainer's films, spoken language, although by no means homogeneous, tends to draw together the collaged fragments which characterise her style, pointing to the presence of a single organising consciousness. Asked about the personal in her work, Rainer admits 'There's a lot of personal material in my films but it's diffused, decentral-ized, contravened by antinarrative techniques' (quoted in MacDonald 1992: 348). The impersonal material in her films is also personal in the sense suggested by Scott MacDonald: it represents her thoughts and interests at any given time (347).

Typically, Rainer's earlier work is constructed as a serial accumulation of segments (a method she miniaturises in the micro-fragments of the sequence 'An Emotional Accretion in 48 Steps' in *Film About a Woman Who...* (1974)). Her later work tends to be organised around a central narrative, which is subject to frequent interruption by the incorporation of other kinds of material: found footage, documentary footage, interviews, intertitles, dream sequences, reflexive shots of the set or crew, and so forth. The use of voice-off is a constant feature throughout her work, and since her first film, its deployment has become gradually more complex. The basic spatial system of Rainer's films is laid out in *Lives of Performers* (1972): the diegesis comprises two spatial planes, one composed of the images (dancers rehearsing and performing, a scrapbook of photographs, typewritten intertitles) and the sync sound which occasionally accom-panies them, the other consisting of an off-screen space from which voices emanate, giving the dancers instructions, narrating and offering commentary and discussion. Although the on-screen performers can address the off-screen space, as when one of them speaks in sync sound straight to camera, this is rare. The voices are identified as belonging to Rainer and the cast, but the nature of their relationship to the images is unclear: is the disjuncture indicative of a temporal gap, a discontinuity in consciousness, a division between performance and reality, or a break between types of performance? Is it all of these things at different times, or indeed, none of them?

In later films, Rainer introduces more variables in the relationships between these planes, and sometimes more planes, but preserves this basic structure, and with it, a tendency to give the last word to the disem-bodied voice-off. This is used to brilliant effect in *The Man Who Envied Women* (1985), where, as Berenice Reynaud has shown (1987), Rainer models heterosexual misrecognition in layered planes: a man, Jack Deller, sits in front of a cinema screen and talks to camera, laying bare his misogyny to an invisible psychoanalyst, while behind him, out of his sightline, clips of Hollywood and avant-garde movies provide a contrapuntal commentary on his discourse; off-screen, the disembodied voice of a woman, Trisha, tells her story, subsuming his, although generally not responding directly to his speech. Rainer builds inequality into the power struggle between the two discourses: Deller is almost always part of the on-screen collage, subject to fragmentation, interruption and discontinuity – he is even played by two dissimilar actors – while Trisha is usually disembodied and aligned with the off-screen power of enunciation. In addition, she is directly associated with Rainer in several ways: her voice is provided by Trisha Brown, but when her body is briefly represented in a dream sequence, she is played by Rainer, and there are several indications that she and Rainer occupy the same off-screen space, as when they are heard together, discussing the press clippings that make up Trisha's political wall collage (although, in a further twist, Rainer is in fact performing the words of Martha Rosler). At different points, Rainer playing herself (or a self) and an actress playing Trisha briefly enter the frame, indicating that the space they inhabit is an envelope rather than a plane, containing all the other diegetic planes.

The Man Who Envied Women has been praised for its dialogism (see Fischer 1989: 301–29), and it does include many different types of quotation, from film clips to cultural theory to quotidian fragments, but the subsumption of these within a single discursive envelope effectively means that no matter how disguised and dispersed Rainer's enunciation, the film is still 'spoken' by her. This is the strength and weakness of Rainer's style: her powerful female voice circumvents the conventions of female objectification, but its disembodied omniscience overrides her strategies of fragmentation, to reinstate discursive hierarchy. The limitations of her approach become clear when she attempts, in *Privilege* (1990), to frame a narrative which can incorporate multiple perspectives. The opening credits describe it as 'a film by Yvonne Rainer and many others', and its complex structure involves multiple envelopes: Rainer's *Privilege* contains fragments of *Privilege* by Yvonne Washington (a putative documentary on menopause directed by a black woman played by Novella Nelson), a fictional flashback narrated by Jenny, one of Washington's (white) interviewees, a commentary on the events in the flashback, given by Digna, a Puerto Rican woman, textual fragments from a wide variety of sources including Frantz Fanon, Eldridge Cleaver and Teresa de Lauretis, along with found footage including old medical films about menopause, and more. The flashback constitutes the film's centre, by virtue of its duration and the complexity of its realisation, placing an anecdote about white complicity and liberal guilt at the heart of the film (the young Jenny perjures herself to ensure the prosecution of her neighbour, Carlos, for the attempted rape of another neighbour, Brenda). Rainer then interrogates this by installing an elaborate point-of-view system which she relates to its title:

> Every character in the film can be seen as either having or not having privilege, depending on race, sex, class, age. If they didn't have it, I gave it *to* them. I privileged Digna to be the commentator, to be more omniscient than Jenny, and to be able to follow Jenny around without being seen. 'Privilege' is a crucial term in the film, a kind of prism through which all these issues – and techniques – can be observed. (Rainer in MacDonald 1992: 352)

The manner in which this is accomplished is ingenious and funny, with Jenny revisiting the scenes of her youth as a menopausal woman, because she cannot be bothered with 'expensive illusionism', and Digna tracking her, unseen despite an outrageous Carmen Miranda costume. At the same time, the notion of handing out privilege smacks of ventriloquism or tokenism, intended to impart 'representativeness' to the text. This implies a literal understanding of dialogism (Fanon is quoted in the film; he doesn't speak in it), which conflicts with Rainer's admission of her authorial prerogative: 'I'm split across any number of people in this film. You might say the whole film goes on in my own head' (quoted in MacDonald 1992: 350). Ultimately, it is not the formal system of *Privilege* that is problematic, but the claims to representativeness made on its behalf, which fly in the face of its multiple inscriptions of *white* authorship. In Patricia Mellencamp's words, the film 'fails to listen and it speaks for others' (1995b: 32; see also Margulies 1996: 104–9). In many other respects, *Privilege* may be Rainer's most formally interesting film, offering a rare instance of feminist 'multiform narrative' (the type of narrative with multilinear plot structures usually but not exclusively found in computer games and interactive media; see McMahan 1999). Rainer's 'distribution and redimensioning of the "I"' (Margulies 1996: 105) is a feminist strategy with two objectives: to re-model female subjectivity, without recourse to the fiction of the unity of the subject, and to invoke collectivity while respecting difference. She succeeds in the first of these, with the creation of an idiosyncratic mode of filmic discourse that is at once radically discontinuous and yet intelligently coherent; her failure in the second objective is a salutary demonstration of the limitations of 'distributed subjectivity' as a strategy for opening democratic dialogue.

Coda: Mona Hatoum's foreign bodies

The kind of experimental film-making practised by Akerman, Rainer and Export in the 1970s and 1980s all but disappeared in the 1990s, but far from marking the obsolescence of their concerns, this signals the extent to which they have been taken up in other forms and other institutional spaces, particularly within the visual arts. Cultural logics and new technologies have played their part in the proliferation of first-person discourses and tropes of self-inscription: discourses of postmodernism have popularised relativistic versions of discursive authority and subjectivity, while digital equipment has greatly increased the accessibility and flexibility of image production. These trends inform a wide range of works by women artists in video and other new media, including those of Sadie Benning, Sophie Calle, Tracey Emin, Joan Jonas, Miranda July, Gillian Wearing and Jane and Louise Wilson.

The proliferation of an experimental trope is usually accompanied by the dissipation of its radicalism and, indeed the trope of self-inscription in contemporary women artists' video generally takes less challenging forms than it does in the films discussed in this chapter. The work of Mona Hatoum is an exception which proves the continued relevance of feminist interrogations of authorship and subjectivity, even as it argues for the necessity of confronting other aspects of the material processes which produce identities and speaking positions.

Most of Hatoum's art deals directly or obliquely with her experience of exile (she was born to a Palestinian family in exile in Lebanon, and has spent most of her adult life in London). The body, as a channel for sensory experience and a reference point in relation to objects and spaces, is often important in her work. The installation *Corps étranger* (1994) seems the ultimate exploration of female authorial embodiment: endoscopic video images of Hatoum's digestive and reproductive tracts are projected onto a circular screen on the floor of a claustrophobic structure resembling a small observatory. Spectators enter the structure and view the screen from its edge, poised above the illusion of a vertiginous fall into someone else's corporeality. Hatoum describes the work as evolving from an interest in surveillance and a fantasy concerning a 'penetrating gaze' which can see through clothes and even flesh:

> I wanted to give the feeling that the body becomes vulnerable in the face of the scientific eye, probing it, invading its boundaries, objec-
> tifying it ... on the other hand, when you enter the room, in places you feel like you are on the edge of an abyss that can swallow you up, the devouring womb, the vagina dentata, castration anxiety ... there is a sense of threat which is something that is present in a lot of my work. (Hatoum in Spinelli, 1997: 138)

The sense of threat which the installation generates is bivalent: the gaze threatens the body, and the body threatens the bearer of the gaze; both or either might represent the 'foreign body' of the title. Hatoum reprises the archetypal scopic shock of Freudian theory (the suppos-edly terrifying sight of female genitalia), and imparts to it an unsettling reciprocity which is partly an effect of the technological uncanny, and partly a displaced expression of the exile's dislocated sense of self and other (though the title is the only tangible indication of this concern): the femininity with which the work engages is not conceptualised abstractly, but is located in a historical matrix as particularly modern and migrant.

Corps étranger complements Hatoum's video, *Measures of Distance* (1988), a cathartic personal work about the effects of exile on her relationship with her mother, in which the emphasis falls on language and separation rather than the body and closeness. Both works extend the feminist inquiry into selfhood in a new direction by registering the experiences of transience and marginality in a globalised culture. As Edward Said says, 'Her work is the presentation of identity as unable to identify with itself, but nevertheless grappling the notion (perhaps only the ghost) of identity to itself' (2000: 17).

3   THE POLITICS OF LOCATION AND DISLOCATION:
WOMEN'S CINEMA AND CULTURAL IDENTITY

It was not enough to say 'As a woman I have no country; as a woman my country is the whole world.' Magnificent as that vision may be, we can't explode into its breadth without a conscious grasp on the particular and concrete meaning of our location here and now. (Adrienne Rich cited in Akomfrah 1989: 5)

Women's cinema and the politics of location

The term 'politics of location' was coined by the feminist writer Adrienne Rich, as a corrective to the white and Western presumptions of main-stream US feminism. In a series of essays written in the 1980s, Rich argues that feminists must abandon their aspirations to universality (represented in the quotation above by Virginia Woolf's words) in order to recognise the cultural differences and inequalities that exist between women (A. Rich 1986). In Rich's understanding, the female condition is neither common nor given, but is produced as a variable effect of inter-secting socio-cultural systems.

The notion of a politics of location has been immensely productive for feminism, but also extremely problematic. In much of the theoretical writing of the 1980s, respect for cultural difference goes hand-in-hand with a disabling relativism. As Fred Pfeil warns: 'The properly ethical concern for serious consideration for other determinate points of view may devolve into an apolitical aesthetic of postmodern delectation in masquerade costume as politics' (1994: 218). Floating free of political responsibility, the fissile rhetoric of difference theory offers no basis for the construction of commonality between the balkanised constituencies of identity politics, no grounds for joining the local to the global. In the 1990s, feminist theorists began to move beyond cultural relativism and political atomisation, influenced by arguments in the new field of cultural geography and analyses of the global cultural economy and geopolitical aesthetics (see Appadurai 1990; Jameson 1992), as well as by the anti-globalisation movement. Inderpal Grewal and Caren Kaplan argue for feminist analyses which ground cultural difference and identity in the complex material conditions of the global economy:

> We know that there is an imperative need to address the concerns of women around the world in the historicized particularity of their relationship to multiple patriarchies as well as to international economic hegemonies ... We need to articulate the relationship of gender to scattered hegemonies such as global economic structures, patriarchal nationalisms, 'authentic' forms of tradition, local structures of domination, and legal-juridical oppression on multiple levels. (1994: 17)

Grewal and Kaplan's priorities include: the interrelations of global and local social organisation, and traditional and modern systems; encounters between mobile capital and multiple subjectivities; the complex relationships between women throughout the world and the possibilities for coalition and affiliation between located feminisms. Like the conjunctural analysis which became so central to the thinking of Claire Johnston, located feminist theory positions femininity as neither an essence nor a discursive effect, but as a geopolitical construct. However, although the notion of located femininities is an effective critical tool for dismantling essentialist conceptions of womanhood, there is always a risk that they will be replaced by ahistorical conceptions of cultural or national identity:

A politics of location is most useful, then, in a feminist context when it is used to deconstruct any dominant hierarchy or hegemonic use of the term gender. A politics of location is not useful when it is construed to be the reflection of authentic, primordial identities that are to be reestablished and reaffirmed. (Kaplan 1994: 139)

In women's cinema, a feminist politics of location is articulated by those films which situate female identity in dynamic historical situations, to reveal the imbrication of technologies of gender with those of local, national and international power. In this chapter, then, I will examine women's filmmaking practices at a variety of specific and located junctures, and will attempt to show, beyond the simple fact of their geographical and historical specificity, some of the ways that their located (and dislocated) aesthetics respond to particular patriarchies and other localised and globalised power relations. As space permits only a brief discussion of each example, the chapter is necessary somewhat fragmentary.

Women's cinema/national cinema

Within Cultural Studies, Benedict Anderson's definition of nation as 'an imagined political community' has provided an invaluable materialist framework for the critical study of national cultures (1991: 6). Anderson and others have drawn attention to the comparative newness of the nation-state and the ways it has been naturalised by nationalist myth. Feminist critics have noted that for women, the sense of belonging thus promoted is usually mediated via a familial imaginary (the practical arrangements for this range from the 'sexual politics' of dynastic marriages which Anderson observes to the more widespread ideological functioning of the family). E. Ann Kaplan states: 'Women do not inhabit a space of the state as home: women rather inhabit a space of their family as home, a space of much more local relations' (1997: 45).

While the general theoretical validity of this statement is rather open to question, it nevertheless offers a recognisable description of the position of women in many societies, and shows how ideologies of gender are imbricated with those of nation. The concrete link between nation and family is patriarchy, a term which designates both a social system and a family structure. In patriarchal culture, the interpellation of female subjects generally involves complex symbolic manoeuvres. As Teresa de Lauretis points out, femininity functions in patriarchy as both sign and value, symbolic abstraction and natural resource (1984: 12–36). As neither aspect of this paradoxical formulation requires a particularly developed social subjectivity, female and feminist cultural production must necessarily engage, at some level, in resistance to interpellation into the nation-as-family. The clearest instance of gendered symbolism in nationalist ideology is the iconic tradition which figures the nation and nationalist struggle as female or maternal (e.g. the Marianne in France, Britannia in the UK). The relationship between female citizens and maternal national imagery can be particularly complex and ambivalent, as Elzbieta Ostrowska (1998) has shown in the case of the nationalist myth of the 'Polish Mother' which exhorts women to make sacrifices for a motherland served by patriarchal institutions. E. Ann Kaplan notes the prevalence and productive ambivalence of films by women which trope national identity in terms of mother-daughter relationships:

> It is no accident that women filmmakers, in turn, work through relations to nation via mother-daughter relations. It is as if they respond within the very position allocated them in national discourse, one relegated to the domestic paradigm, but use that position for resistance. (1997: 50)

However, films like Chantal Akerman's *News from Home*, Su Friedrich's *The Ties That Bind* (1984) and Martine Attille's *Dreaming Rivers* (1988), which approach questions of cultural transmission via mother-daughter relationships, often do so in order to retrieve or retain a culture which has been or may be lost or modified by exile, migration or separation. Conversely, when feminist filmmakers represent state power and its effects on women's lives, it is more common for them to focus on the institutions of patriarchy.

To illustrate some of the ways that women filmmakers have explored, rejected and reworked interpellation into the nation-as-family, I shall examine two brief examples of practices of women's cinema in relation to their contexts, namely the *Frauenfilm* in New German Cinema and women's film in the Iranian New Wave. Although widely separated by time, culture and geography, these two examples are not without parallels, and serve, moreover, to emphasise the fact that the concept of located cultural politics is as relevant to white Western Europe as it is to the rest of the world.

New German Cinema and the Frauenfilm

New German Cinema began in the Federal Republic in the 1960s with the rebellion of a generation of young and almost exclusively male directors against the poverty of their national film culture. Women did not make a significant impact within the movement until the late 1970s, but by the 1980s, West Germany had 'proportionally more women film-makers than any other film-producing country' (Elsaesser 1989: 185). Julia Knight argues that reliance on public subsidy excluded women for the first ten years, then constrained them to work within documentary and topic-based fiction around 'women's issues', in addition to which, the small budgets they were given worked against the achievement of high production values, fuelling scepticism about women's technical proficiency (1992). The activist orientation of the women's movement also favoured the production of documentaries and campaigning films rather than auteurist fictions.

However, although women were scarcely involved in the *Autorenkino* or 'author's cinema' of the 1960s and early 1970s, the films of Alexander Kluge, the movement's leading figure, are populated by restless and alienated female protagonists who function as bell-wethers of a generation.[1] This allegorical tendency intersected with the feminist impulse to personal-political testimony, and was given an institutional outlet in *das kleine Fernsehspiel* (the small television play), the late night film slot of the television channel ZDF, which aimed to create a 'forum for witnesses to the age'.[2] The *Frauenfilm* (women's film) emerged from the encounter of the women's movement and the New German Cinema, and although, as Knight points out, it was neither homogeneous nor the sole arena of women's contributions, it did give rise to a distinct and powerful structure of feeling, of historic significance within both women's cinema and German film culture.

Public funding freed filmmakers from the constraints of commercial cinema, as Ulrike Sieglohr puts it: 'In effect, the New German Cinema functioned in West Germany throughout the 1970s primarily as a public sphere – a forum for debating contemporary issues – rather than within the realm of entertainment' (1998: 467). This debate revolved around German national identity, both during and since World War Two. The women's film's relationship with historical and political questions was oblique for a number of reasons. The rise of the ultra-left and the activities of terrorists in the 1970s were met with such a draconian response by the government that by the end of the decade talk of a police state was not unrealistic. The dual orientation of feminism, towards an international women's movement on the one hand, and towards the small-scale politics of the personal on the other, gave women a unique political vantage point in the aftermath of 1968. As Thomas Elsaesser puts it: 'Directly exposed to a double oppression and experiencing their social role as marginal, women seemed in a better position than male heterosexual Marxists to keep intact the hopes of social change and the revolutionary ideals of the anti-authoritarian movement' (1989: 184).

Instead of a direct political critique, many of the most powerful films of the period displaced resistance into accounts of individual psychological and physical crises. Filmmakers turned to the years of their own childhood and adolescence in search of the causes of their own rebellion and the repression of the 1970s. They saw in the economic miracle of Germany's recovery in the 1950s a corrupt materialism, paid for with the distorting effects of political amnesia. *Hunger Years* (*Hungerjahre*, Jutta Brückner, 1980) and *No Mercy, No Future* (*Die Berührte*, Helma Sander-Brahms, 1981) offer brutal and terrifying portrayals of adolescents precipitated into breakdowns by the coldness of their families and the anomic society that surrounds them. In these films anorexia, bulimia, psychosis, joyless promiscuity, abortion and attempted suicide are the stations of a *via dolorosa* to abjection, which in Sanders-Brahms' film, the more expressionistic of the two, is explicitly related to the crucifixion.

The political significance of these intense personal dramas is communicated through mise-en-scène. For instance, in an early scene in *No Mercy, No Future*, the heroine strips naked and lies in the snow beside an army firing range; towards the end of the film, walking beside the Berlin Wall, she passes graffiti which says 'Madness'. The wall is also important in Helke Sanders's *Redupers* (1977), where it signifies not schizophrenia but the more prosaically divided self of the working mother. Margarethe von Trotta's *German Sisters* (*Die Bleierne Zeit*, 1981) deals directly with the political events of the 1970s, basing its story of two sisters fairly closely on the life and death in prison of Gudrun Ensslin of the Baader-Meinhof group, as told to von Trotta by Ensslin's sister. The film's commitment to the facts and its survivor's perspective make it sober rather than grim, but it does share some of the imagery of the other films previously discussed. Horror at the unspoken sins of the older generation takes the form of a physical response when one of the sisters vomits at a school screening of the Holocaust documentary *Night and Fog* (*Nuit et brouillard*, 1956), shown in a flashback to the 1950s. Merging and splitting, which connote madness and death in the other films, are touched upon in the imagery of doubling and division which von Trotta skilfully weaves between the sisters.

What is shared by the films in this cycle is a unique perspective on German history, understood in terms of the relationship between the body and the state. The body is at once the source of our first and most inalienable sense of self-possession, and, at the same time, an object over which the state has absolute power. Brückner, Sanders-Brahms and von Trotta explore this relationship at a number of levels: in the indirect exercise of state power over the body through the family; in the direct and brutal enactment of that power through institutions such as prison or the mental hospital; in the postulation of a psychosomatic conversion of repressed historical traumas into mental and physical pathology; and in the elaboration of an aesthetic based on that conversion.

Juliet Mitchell argues that evidence of hysteria in the children of Holocaust survivors suggests that 'an actual trauma in one generation may not be induced until the next, when it may be lived as hysteria' and that this may constitute a social phenomenon as much as an individual plight (2000: 280). The fantasmatic emergence of historical issues in New German Cinema suggests that something similar could be said of Holocaust guilt. In the women's film, the identification of femininity with the body and the feminisation of certain psychopathologies are turned to account in the visceral excavation of personal and national identity.

Women directors in the Iranian New Wave

The Iranian New Wave began in 1969, with Dariush Mehrju'i's *The Cow* (*Gav*), but the national industry suffered an economic decline in the 1970s and was subject to virulent attacks in the Revolution of 1979, when cinemas were burned and many filmmakers fled into exile. The new regime purged the industry of its 'corrupting' elements and enforced regulations codifying 'Islamic values', paying particular attention to modesty conventions governing the veiling of women and contact between the sexes. Initially, women disappeared from films, as filmmakers were uncertain about what was allowed.

The regulation of the industry brought images of women back to the screen, although their roles were circumscribed in ways that favoured moralistic idealisation. Bahram Baiza'i's *Bashu, the Little Stranger* (*Bashu, gharibeh-ye kuchak*, 1985) exemplifies this trend, with its depiction of two powerful maternal presences, one living and one dead. The film centres on a mother who defies the xenophobia of the family and community to care for a dark-skinned boy from southern Iran who has been orphaned by the war with Iraq. Bashu is also watched over by his dead mother who makes several ghostly appearances, silent and heavily veiled. In *Bashu*, a symptomatisation of the idealisation of women occurs: the ambiguous and negative aspects of the maternal which have been expunged from the film's heroine return in the uncanny figure of the ghost mother, who functions as a reminder and harbinger of loss.

'Islamic values' also brought new formal conventions, as Hamid Naficy explains:

A new grammar for filming developed, involving shot composition, acting, touching and relay of the gaze between male and female actors. In essence, this grammar encouraged a 'modesty of looking and acting' and instituted an 'averted look' instead of the direct gaze, particularly one imbued with desire. (1996: 676–7)

Paradoxically, the 'purification' of the cinema made filmmaking into a suitable profession for women, and as the New Wave reached maturity it brought almost a dozen women to prominence as directors of features (a larger number than in most Western countries). These women are active in both of the types of filmmaking which have evolved in Iran, the popular (national) cinema which operates within (and debates) post-revolutionary Islamic values and the art (international) cinema which addresses its criticisms of those values to a cultural elite within and outside Iran.

The country's most successful woman director, Rakhshan Bani-Etemad, has worked effectively within the popular cinema as well as receiving recognition internationally. Her work explores and stretches the boundaries of the possible under censorship. The principal problem for Iranian filmmakers representing private life is the understanding of cinematic images as part of the public sphere: female characters are veiled not from the diegetic looks of the other characters, but from the gaze of male spectators. Along with the prohibition of physical contact and the direct representation of sexuality, this distorts the depiction of everyday life.

In *The May Lady* (*Banu-ye Ordibehesht*, 1997) Bani-Etemad breaks taboos on subject matter with the story of a female documentary director (Minoo Farshi) who is a divorced single mother with a lover. Bani-Etemad works around the taboo on the representation of the lovers' relationship by completely avoiding visual representation of the man.[3] Instead of meeting in person, the characters talk intimately on the telephone, exchange letters and quote Persian poetry to one another. The two voices are interwoven in a displaced representation of sexual love, which is anchored diegetically in a female perspective. The incorporation of censorship requirements thus gives rise to an acoustic poetry of female desire. In contrast to this lyricism, the protagonist's motherhood leads her to confront sexual segregation more directly, when her son is arrested for attending a party where both sexes are present. A concern with mothers is embedded in the film as a reflexive discourse through the protagonist's work on a documentary about motherhood, fragments of which are included in the film. The film's relationship to censorship restrictions is encapsulated by one celebrated image: although the protagonist is seen wearing the veil, even in her home, there is one shot in which she reaches up to remove it as she passes through her bedroom door. At this moment, Bani-Etemad cuts, unmistakably signalling the existence of a reality which is just out of view. The emphasis on the negotiation of restrictions and conventions, in society and in cinema, which characterises Bani-Etemad's work is consistent with its address to a national audience, and places its concerns in the context of women's struggles within Iran.

Marzieh Meshkini's *The Day I Became a Woman* (*Rouzi Ke Zan Shodam*, 2000) is an example of the Iranian art cinema. Made for the production house founded by her husband, the prolific director Mohsen Makhmalbaf, who is also father to the young director Samira Makhmalbaf, the film presents three stories about the meaning of womanhood at three stages of life: childhood, young adulthood, and old age. It is set on the island of Kish, in southern Iran, a beautiful location with a holiday atmosphere which the film exploits. The title comes from the first story, of a girl on her ninth birthday, the day on which, according to tradition, she must begin veiling herself and stop playing with boys. She negotiates with her mother and grandmother and wins herself one hour's freedom until the exact time of her birth. Her male friend cannot come out to play, so they share a lollipop through a barred window.[4] The heroine of the second story is part of a large group of women in chadors taking part in a cycle race on a seaside road.[5] Her husband and all her other male relatives chase her on horses, threatening her with divorce and exclusion for her indecorum. In the third story, an elderly wheelchair-bound woman hires a young boy to take her on a spending spree. In a shiny shopping mall, she buys furniture, white goods and everything needed to set up home, blowing an inheritance on the luxuries she has longed for all her life.

In common with other Iranian art films, *The Day I Became a Woman* sweetens its ironies with striking images and gorgeous colour. The first story begins with an indecipherable image of light through mesh on a screen divided into four by a cross; its final shot reveals that the mesh is the young girl's veil, which she has given to some boys to use as a sail on a home-made boat. The second and third stories are structured as supports for surreal visual incongruity which, in the style of several contemporary Iranian women artists, derives from the juxtaposition of modernity and tradition. The final story ends when the old lady returns to the mall for something she has forgotten, and the neighbourhood boys unpack her purchases and set up home on the beach. The still image used on the poster for the film's UK screenings shows a double bed with theatrical white curtains and a white wedding dress displayed against a background of stripes of blue sky, green sea and golden sand. The foreground juxtaposes this luxury wedding night scenario with a figure wrapped in a huge printed veil – actually a boy with his face concealed. The image embodies the bizarre cultural clashes between dreams of femininity and the reality of womanhood for someone old enough to have experienced both Westernisation and Islamicisation.

Although Meshkini's film has been described as 'allegorical', its meanings are elided as much as coded: as in other films from the House of Makhmalbaf, dazzling colour and bold composition form a tactical display of beauty which distracts from the details of the film's social critique. As political cinema, Meshkini's film is in some ways more challenging, and in other ways more oblique than *The May Lady*. Its meaningful gaps invite political commentary from audiences drawn from the international liberal intelligentsia. The risk which this incurs is that the film is also liable to reinscription within other, possibly anti-Islamic, political agendas.

If the veiling of meaning seems characteristic of liberal women's cinema in Iran, it is because its existence is extremely precarious. This was demonstrated by the arrest, in August 2001, of the director Tahmineh Milani for allegedly supporting 'counter revolutionary' groups in her film *The Hidden Half* (2001). Unlike Bani-Etemad and others who distance themselves from feminism, Milani is known for her feminist views. Her arrest highlights the particular dangers faced by Iranian filmmakers in a country where the secular parliament works under a religious leader and where the judiciary is also religious. Films pass through a complex process of script approval and censorship by the reformist Culture Ministry, but this apparent government sanction may not protect filmmakers from the courts and their power to impose brutal sentences. At the time of writing, Milani has been released on bail, but will be tried on charges for which the most severe sentence could be execution.

Feminism and post-colonialism

For many women filmmakers, cultural identity is as dislocated as it is located, deterritorialised by histories of migration, colonisation and exile as well as by patriarchal exclusion, and filmmaking for them is a doubly minor practice. Ella Shohat argues that post-colonial women's cinema challenges both feminism and post-colonialism, refusing the universalising discourses of the women's movement in the 1970s and correcting the lack of attention to gender in post-war anti-colonial movements and the cultural discourses, including Third Cinema, that flowed from them. In most anti-colonial struggles, sexual equality has been relegated to the bottom of the agenda, a detail to be addressed after the more pressing issue of establishing the nation. Consequently, many post-colonial nations have carried forward the gender relations of earlier eras. Post-colonial women's films, Shohat claims, 'challenge the masculinist contours of the "nation" in order to continue a feminist decolonization of Third-Worldist historiography, as much as they continue a multicultural decolonization of feminist historiography' (Shohat 1997).

The work of Moufida Tlatli is particularly interesting for its rigorous working through of a female perspective on colonial and post-colonial society in formal systems drawn from melodrama (of the Egyptian rather than Hollywood variety, as Laura Mulvey points out (1995)). The hallmarks of melodrama, including non-verbalisation, musical self-expression, spatial enclosure and conversion hysteria have become signatures of Tlatli's style in her first two films. Her powerful imagery explores the ways colonialism and sexism are interiorised, within the home, the family, the self and the body.

Moufida Tlatli: The Silences of the Palace

Moufida Tlatli worked as an editor for twenty years, cutting films for some of the most important directors of the Mahgreb cinema, before making her debut as a director. Tlatli belongs to the first generation of women in Tunisia to experience relative freedom. After independence was achieved in 1956, the secular regime outlawed polygamy and the veil, allowed women to enter the professions and even legalised abortion. However, many aspects of women's roles were not transformed: 'Traditionally in the Arab film world, a girl works in continuity or editing. I had never thought of making films. I loved editing' (Tlatli in Lennon 2001: 11). She cites a seven-year period spent caring for her two children and her mother who suffered from Alzheimer's as the catalyst of her directing career, and although her work is not autobiographical, the intensity with which she addresses the situation of Tunisian women suggests historical inquiry galvanised by personal experience and empathy with her mother's generation.

The Silences of the Palace (Saimt el qusur, 1994) is a revisionist film in two senses. Firstly, it questions the discourses of nationalism and unity which, in the Third Cinema of the 1960s, tended to foreclose discussion of the place of women in colonial or post-colonial society. Secondly, it employs a melodramatic mode previously rejected by liberationist filmmakers in the Arab countries reacting against the imported aesthetics of American and Indian films. Tlatli, one of several women directors who have risen to prominence at a time of crisis in Tunisian cinema, sees her work as part of a populist revaluation of the Egyptian melodrama of the 1950s, which she describes as 'a cinema of excess' (Mulvey 1995: 18).

The bulk of the film consists of flashbacks leading up to a narrative climax set against the events of 1956 (the year in which Tunisia won its independence from France) embedded in a framing narrative set in the mid-1960s. The story concerns an unsuccessful singer, Alia (Hend Sabri in the flashback and Ghalia Lacroix in the diegetic present), who performs in restaurants for family functions and lives in sin with a middle-class intellectual who refuses to marry her because of her low social status. At the start of the film, we learn that she is pregnant and planning an abortion which will not be her first. News of the death of Sidi Ali, a Bey prince in whose household she grew up, sends her back to the palace and precipitates the flashback. In the palace sequences, it becomes clear that Alia is the illegitimate daughter of Sidi Ali and Khedija (Ahmel Hedhili), a servant. By confining the flashbacks to the palace, rigidly codified as the spaces occupied by the royal family (upstairs) and their servants (downstairs), Tlatli suggests the introversion of a ruling class on the brink of losing its power and the occlusion of the women immured and enslaved in their household. Tlatli endows the scenes of the women's lives in the kitchen with communitarian warmth as well as stifling oppression. Long takes show them laughing and singing together, and dialogue is often structured with the communality of a chorus. At the same time the enclosed space, outside of which there is nothing for the women but prostitution or worse, is a pressure cooker for their frustrated longings. As news of the unrest on the streets of Tunis reaches the kitchen via radio broadcasts, it triggers an outburst in which one woman speaks, as in a trance, from an interior self as distant as the barricades: 'We have nothing to be afraid of. I don't belong to myself. I want to go out in the street to run unhindered, naked and barefoot, and scream and shout out loud. Only their bullets can silence me as they run through me, turning my body into a sieve.' The desperate lyricism of her speech founders on the image of her body as a kitchen implement, returning her to a seemingly inescapable fate.

Alia's upbringing in the palace is represented as a quest for identity. Twice she demands that her mother tell her who her father is. Born on the same day as Sarra, the daughter of Sidi Ali's brother, she grows up alongside her and follows her like a shadow. Her position is spelled out in a sequence in which 'the family' has a formal group photograph taken: Alia follows Sarra into the frame, and is asked by the photographer to step aside. As well as attempting to establish her legitimacy by being seen, Alia tries to discover the truth about her origins by looking. Violating the division between upstairs and downstairs, Alia explores the palace and spies on the adults. Several times she is seen gazing at her own face in a mirror, as if to discern her identity there. Alia's family romance, her search for a father who will help her avoid her mother's fate, comes to an end when her adolescent beauty and musical talents are noticed by the men upstairs, and they begin asking for her to entertain and serve them. Khedija protects her, but is raped and made pregnant by Sidi Ali's brother as a result, and Alia transfers her hopes to another man, Lotfi, the nationalist tutor of the Bey children. The climax of the film draws its themes together in an extraordinary narrative crisis. The possibility that Alia will be placed in the same position as her mother is realised in a striking sequence in which Tlatli shows Khedija seated before a full-length mirror, putting on make-up before going to wait on the family. Alia, seen only in the mirror, stands behind her. After Khedija explains that they want her to sing upstairs, Alia takes her mother's place before the mirror, with her mother behind her, in a perfect rhyme with the earlier shot. Soon after this, Khedija reveals to Alia that the reason they have no family is because she was sold to the Bey as a child. With melodramatic synchronicity, at the moment of the Tunisian uprising, Alia causes outrage at Sarra's engagement party, where she has been asked to perform, by singing a forbidden nationalist anthem and Khedija dies as a result of a self-induced miscarriage. At the film's close, Alia is seen in a marginally-improved situation, but Tlatli makes it clear that Tunisia's independence has not brought freedom or justice for women: most of the old servants remain in the palace, Alia works for her living, but in a profession which gives her little more status than a prostitute, and Lotfi, for all his revolutionary ideals, is not prepared to marry a woman without a respectable family behind her. The film ends with Alia deciding to keep her child, and, if it is a girl, to name her Khedija: she realises that her search for an identity through patriarchy has been a mistake, and that her mother's courage is all she can inherit from her family.

The use of melodrama, with its oppositions, coincidences, silences and displacements makes the film simultaneously highly schematic and intensely emotional, while its intricate exploration of looking relations and its rigorous systems of imagery (mirrors, music, enclosure) give it a remarkable aesthetic coherence. Embedded in these metaphoric and metonymic systems is an uncompromising historical argument. Tlatli shows how anti-colonial struggle fails to take account of the gender-

FIGURE 5 *Silences of the Palace*

specific oppressions of working class women. By focusing on the women, leaving both colonialists and nationalists off-screen, Tlatli inverts the rhetoric of most political cinema, setting the scene for political struggle not in the street, but in the closed, interior spaces of the home.

Tlatli's second film, *La Saison des hommes* (1999), deals again with homosocial female spaces, but regards these much more critically. Set on the island of Djerba, where women live apart from their men for eleven months of the year, the film shows a version of traditional family life in which patriarchal social rules are enforced tyrannically on behalf of the absent husbands by their mothers. Despite the centrality of mother-daughter relationships to Tlatli's work, femininity is represented as a shifting construct defined in relation to family, nation, tradition and modernity, never a timeless essence to be sentimentalised.

White directors and post-colonialism: The Piano and Chocolat

In discussing feminism and post-colonialism, it is important to distin-guish the different positions occupied by women within power relations

FIGURE 6   *Silences of the Palace*

of colonialism, and to delineate the ways that their struggles are inflected by their positioning. The question of white women directors' relationship with post-colonialism impinges on a number of difficult questions, concerning the extent and nature of women's complicity and culpability in colonialism, the ways that white femininity signifies in racist ideology, and the meanings which white women have projected onto the colonised landscape and indigenous people. The distinction between colonial powers such as Britain and settler nations such as Australia or New Zealand adds a further complication, which is overlaid with the economic power relations of globalisation. In short, there are rarely only two sides to questions of post-colonial race/gender relations.

All of these issues are relevant to Jane Campion's *The Piano* (1993), a canonical feminist film which has been widely discussed within two frames of reference: as women's romantic fiction and as a post-colonialist representation of colonial New Zealand. Critical responses were generally enthused by the film's construction of female desire, although some dissenters have commented on its sadomasochistic dynamics.[6] A smaller group of critics have interrogated its depiction of cultural identity in relation to contemporary debates in New Zealand. The film's narrative is too well-known to require re-telling here; it is sufficient to note that the story of a bartered bride who takes control of her own destiny has been seen as a feminist fairy tale (specifically, a new version of *Blue-beard*, which it stages *en-abîme*), a gothic romance in the tradition of Emily Brontë, and an allegory of female desire. Lynda Dyson pinpoints the source of its troubling cultural politics in the relationship between narration and setting: 'Romantic melodrama ... set in a landscape where "natives" provide the backdrop for the emotional drama of the principal white characters' (1995: 268). Wildness is central to *The Piano*'s romanticism, as it is to *Wuthering Heights*, with which it has often been compared. Its narrative and imagery are built on a matrix of familiar oppositions: culture/nature, civilised/primitive, male/female. The Maoris signify positively, but they are scarcely individuated; they are not much more than a production value. Dyson argues that their ideological role is to facilitate a 'fantasy of colonial reconciliation':

> Primitivism provides the means to deal with the contradictions of white settler colonialism; while the white colonizers saw themselves bringing progress and civilization to these 'pre-modern' cultures, their project was also energized by the utopian fantasy of building a society free of the political and economic divisions and inequalities of Europe. (268)

This project is condensed in the image of Baines (Harvey Keitel), whose low class status, identification with the Maoris and the land, and sympathy with femininity position him as a mediating figure between oppositions. Baines represents the white New Zealander as *pakeha*, a Maori term meaning outsiders, applied to those with European ancestry, but increasingly used by whites themselves to signify belonging. Dyson argues that *pakeha* have appropriated the ideal of biculturalism, enshrined in the Treaty of Waitangi, despite reneging on the treaty's territorial provisions. The aesthetics of *The Piano* display a comparable sleight of hand: Stewart's propriety and aggressivity, Ada's pallor, her cultured hairstyle, the bourgeois refinement of the piano itself, contrast with the Maori's dark skins, dishevelled appearance and sexual frankness. Even the lighting follows this pattern, foregrounding Ada's blue-white skin against the dark vegetation and rendering Maori faces part of the background obscurity. The scene in which the Maoris, failing to understand theatrical illusion, intervene in the *Bluebeard* play in an attempt to rescue the woman, has been much discussed. The charge of primitivist caricature has been countered by the claim that the film sides with fantasy (Mellencamp 1995a: 182), yet there can be no question as to whose fantasy takes centre-stage. Through its turbulent enactment Ada and Baines reinvent themselves: at the film's end, they move to a nice, clean suburb, where they live as legitimate white New Zealanders.

Annie Goldson makes a significant modification to Dyson's argument, pointing out that the film's own national identity is questionable. The director is an expatriate New Zealander, its two biggest stars North American and, in the absence of New Zealand investment, it has put next to nothing back into the national economy. Goldson agrees with Dyson that the film's reconciliation transforms the principal characters from migrants to settlers, from colonists to *pakeha*, at the expense of the Maori, but argues that this vision of white hegemony is not a reflection of contemporary *pakeha* cultural politics, but a construction imposed from outside, a globalised vision, as it were, of issues local to New Zealand. She notes that in New Zealand, the film's reception was markedly uneasy, especially among progressive *pakeha* who support recent Maori challenges to white land ownership made on the basis of the Treaty of Waitangi, which has the status of a constitutional document: 'The marginalization of the Maori does not reflect a climate that has made a revisiting of the Treaty of Waitangi possible' (1997: 281). In short, the reconciliation which the film effects is at odds with the terms on which biculturalism might really be negotiated.

Whilst an analysis of *The Piano* from the perspective of post-colonial cultural politics may not entirely invalidate the claims made for the film's representation of female subjectivity *in extremis*, it does point to the dangers of over-valuing female desire, making an abstract principle of it, or reducing feminism to its legitimation. The exhilaration felt by feminist film-goers at the extravagant vision of a grand piano carried from one side of the world to the other, from beach to bush and back again, for a wilful woman who prefers its voice to her own, is tempered by an interest in those who have to carry it.

For white feminists, post-colonialism brings the challenge of thinking about sexual difference in relation to cultural difference, engaging with two intersecting sets of power relations without turning one into a metaphor for the other. In *Chocolat* (1988), the French director Claire Denis envisages the white woman's relationship with post-colonialism in terms that are diametrically opposed to Campion's: she explores colonial relationships in their raw immediacy and finds no easy possibility of reconciliation. Denis' film is set in the former French colony of Cameroon. Her protagonist, a white woman allegorically named 'France', is revisiting her childhood home. A long flashback to the 1950s details the complex and ambivalent relationships in the family's colonial household, which centre on the African houseboy, Protée (Isaach de Bankolé). As a child, France mixes with the black servants and is Protée's constant companion. By showing the two eating insects together, Denis depicts the relationship as collusive and illicit. Protée is also the object of other kinds of attention from whites, including an advance made by France's beautiful mother, which he repudiates. E. Ann Kaplan's (1997) analysis of the film centres on inter-racial looking relations, which Denis thematises in Protée's oscillation between hyper-visibility as an object of desire (making a point of de Bankolé's exceptional good looks) and invisibility as a 'native houseboy'. Several scenes show Protée's humiliation, which is linked, in the manner described by Fanon, to his sense of his own physicality and masculinity. When France and her mother walk past him chatting without noticing that, a few feet away, he is washing himself in the outdoor shower used by the servants, he breaks down and weeps.

Towards the conclusion of the film, he ends his friendship with France by hurting them both, tricking her into burning her hand on the generator by placing his own hand there first, in denial of its intense heat. Kaplan says: 'Both the colonized and the women colonizers become subjectivities-in-between, both irrevocably changed by their interaction in the new space within which they live and work because of imperialism' (167). Denis situates these changes in the register of displacement and loss:

Protée's internalisation of colonial values seems to destroy him and France becomes a wanderer who desires what she cannot have. This is grasped by another in-between character in the contemporary framing narrative, William J. Park, an American black man who gives her a lift in his car and offers to read her palm. In her scarred hand he sees no past and no future. She asks him to go for a drink with her, and he laughingly refuses. The film's final shot, framed with immense care, shows African men in post-colonial Cameroon as France sees them: standing by a verdant field of crops, three airport workers on a break talk, laugh and smoke. The camera keeps a respectful distance, and the men's speech is unheard on the soundtrack, as Abdullah Ibrahim's upbeat *African Marketplace* plays the film out. After the preceding exploration of the black male body as an object of the desiring gaze of whites, the film's concluding shot seems to represent the refusal of that gaze and the particular looking relations in which it originates, by a new generation who are not caught up in the destructive effects of colonialism. In contrast to Campion, then, Denis confronts directly the ways that colonialism fosters difference within the self and desire for the 'Other', and concedes the difficulty of reconciliation.

Accented cinema: hybridity, diaspora and exile

In cultural theory, a number of attempts have been made to conceptualise relations across the division that *Chocolat* insists upon, to progress beyond the inter-racial stand-off of cultural nationalism. Trinh T. Minh-ha's work in film and in theory on the notion of the 'Inappropriate(d) Other' undertakes a philosophical deconstruction of the binary categories of 'I' and 'Other' in ethnographic discourse (see Trinh 1989). Many less theoretical filmmakers, such as Gurinder Chadha, or Mira Nair, have used their own experience of hyphenated identity or mobility between cultures as the basis of dramas of cultural difference which insist on its presence *within* communities, families and individuals. The huge range and variety of cinema which operates in between cultures or in several cultures simultaneously has been categorised and mapped by Hamid Naficy as 'accented cinema' (2001). Like women's cinema, accented cinema is unified in diversity: 'The variations among the films are driven by many factors, while their similarities stem principally from what the filmmakers have in common: liminal subjectivity and interstitial location in society and the film industry' (10). Naficy's mapping is useful in avoiding vague 'melting pot' rhetoric, and I have used several of his categories below, without sticking precisely to his taxonomy.

Tracey Moffatt: hybridity

Night Cries: A Rural Tragedy (1989), directed by the Australian artist Tracey Moffatt, is exemplary of hybridity in every way: a theatrical, painterly and cinematic staging of identity at a crossroads where 'the assimilationist narrative has been eviscerated; but there is no utopian multicultural narrative to take its place' (Julien & Nash 1998: 18). The historical context for an understanding of *Night Cries* is the Australian government's policy between the 1930s and the 1970s of the assimilation of Aborigines, pursued through the fostering and adoption of Aboriginal children by white families, often without the informed consent of their parents. The mixed-race relationships thus domesticated all the internal tensions of colonialism, recasting them in terms of familial interdependence. The film envisages an inter-racial mother-daughter relationship in which the passage of time has reversed the direction of dependence: the elderly white mother is cared for by her adopted Aboriginal daughter. In the feminist tradition of the radical remake, Moffatt's film is a revisionist sequel to a classic of Australian cinema, Charles Chauvel's *Jedda* (1955), an overblown Technicolor melodrama about a young Aboriginal woman who lives with a family of white cattle farmers but goes fatally astray, led back to the bush by her attraction to an unassimilated Aboriginal man who awakens her tribal feelings. Although Chauvel's film is liberal for its time, its essentialist version of ethnic identity is unquestionably racist by today's standards; part of Moffatt's project is to complicate the earlier film's conceptualisation of ethnic identity. *Night Cries* has an additional, more personal, context for Moffatt: her own experience as an Aboriginal girl with a white foster mother.

Assimilation informs the aesthetic of the film as well as its politics (see Jayamanne 1992). The mise-en-scène is highly stylised and vividly coloured, the artifice of its studio setting not disguised but foregrounded by smooth shiny surfaces and exquisite modulations of light. Moffatt stages tableaux which employ a stereotypical iconography of the out- back: red earth, clear blue sky and a corrugated iron outhouse. The art direction is influenced by the visual style of Aboriginal painter Albert Namatjira, a popular watercolourist spurned by the critical establish- ment for his lack of 'primitive' authenticity. However, the film's most con- densed image of assimilation is the singer, Jimmy Little, who performs the number that made him a one-hit wonder in 1964, *Royal Telephone*. Little figures in the film as an anachronism, a poignant image of a past concep- tion of successful integration: the lyrics of his song, about telephoning Jesus, his sports jacket and tie, his performance style are 'pure cornball' (91). His appearances are cut into the film so as to juxtapose two oppos- ing visions of assimilation, 'mission school' repression and the raw rela- tions of power and dependency.[7] But the significance of Namatjira and Little goes beyond allegorising or ironising assimilation: as Aboriginal artists in the cultural marketplace they are Moffatt's own precursors, as she carves out a space for herself as an avant-garde artist who engages with popular and mass cultural forms (and who is definitively *not* an Aboriginal spokesperson).

The emotional centre of gravity of *Night Cries* is the mother/daughter drama. In their stylised setting, the bodies of the actors who play the pair seem unbearably real, the mother weightless and brittle, the middle- aged daughter ballasted by her own solidity. The daughter cares for the mother, pushing her wheelchair to the outhouse and washing her feet, but also subjects her to careless cruelties. Their mutual brutalisation is ritualised in a scene in which the daughter cracks a whip outside the win- dow, and indoors, the mother cries out, ambiguously, in pleasure or pain. A flashback shows the relationship's first dynamics, when the daughter, as a child, is left by the mother to play with two Aboriginal boys on the beach. Covered in seaweed by the boys, the terrified child cries out to her mother but her voice is drowned out by the sounds of waves and gulls. Shots of the mother's motionless back, and, in a brilliant edit, one shot from which the mother is absent, are powerfully evocative of childhood fears of abandonment. These fears return in the film's final shot, which shows the mother lying dead and the daughter curled foetally beside her, while the soundtrack of babies' cries and the beating heart of an unborn child heard via ultrasound adds to the confounding of birth, death and abandonment. The mother's death is the occasion of the daughter's rebirth, but it brings with it night terrors of inconsolable loss.

Night Cries allegorises post-colonial identity as the hybrid outcome of a forced filiation, remaking maternal melodrama as '*King Lear* for women ... the tragedy of national history' (Mellencamp 1995a: 266). Whether or not the film qualifies formally as a tragedy, Moffatt's use of the term is interesting: tragedy is a transitional form which mediates between two systems of thought, and is characterised by the presence of irreducible ambivalence. The cultural hybridity which her film concerns and creates resembles tragic ambivalence in its presentation of elements which can neither be separated nor synthesised, but which cleave together and apart, at a moment of transition between two worldviews.[8] In a recent photo series, *Up in the Sky* (1997), Moffatt takes inspiration from Pier Paolo Pasolini's *Accattone* (1961), producing enigmatic pictures which, like his film, achieve their effects through an aesthetic of 'contamination' (*contaminazione*), a linguistic concept used by Pasolini to describe the action of different textual elements on one another in which neither element loses its identity, but their encounter generates something new. As Moffatt's work has developed, her tragic perception of hybridity has been superseded by a vision of a new and strange culturally-mixed milieu, as if, beyond mourning for the divided self, she has created and populated a world of possibilities from the relations between its different parts.

Julie Dash: diaspora

Loss of home and cultural integrity are similarly important to Julie Dash's work, but as the effects of a very different history, that of the African diaspora in the US. *Daughters of the Dust* (1991) is a landmark film which, as Toni Cade Bambara (1993) has shown, offers both a summing up and a signpost for African-American independent film. Dash emerged from the

Los Angeles school of filmmakers who rebelled against the film school curriculum at UCLA in the early 1970s. Bambara notes that *Daughters of the Dust* can be read as a capsule history of African-American independent film since the Los Angeles insurgence, carrying forward its themes and representational strategies, and casting actors whose presence resonates with past roles. African-American women's literature is also an influence, particularly the work of Paule Marshall (*Praise Song for the Widow*) and Toni Morrison (*Beloved*). Ideas of collective identity and spiritual home supply the film's 'unabashedly Afrocentric thesis in the teeth of current-day criticisms of essentialism' (129).

The film is set at Ibo Landing in the South Carolina Sea Islands in 1902. During the slave trade, these islands were a staging post for slaving ships, but their difficult terrain also became a haven where Africans and indigenous Americans could evade persecution. Ibo landing is known for the myth of the Ibos, who were captured and brought to the islands on slave-ships. It is said that when they saw what the Europeans had in store for them, they turned around and walked on top of the water back to their homeland. Now, in the film's time, the islands are home to the emancipated families of the slaves, although a new wave of migration is about to take them north, to the cities. Dash depicts a family, the Peazants, getting together for a reunion before most of them leave for the North. The film takes place on a single day, but uses its narrative structure and the concerns of the characters to argue the value of the past in the construction and retention of a culture which safeguards collective identity for the future.

A spectrum of possible relationships to the past is exemplified by the women of the Peazant family: Nana Peazant is a living link with the past, remembering slavery, honouring her ancestors and practising old ways; Haagar wants to cut ties to the past and seek a new future in the North; Yellow Mary and Viola return from the mainland for the reunion, the former having lost her respectability and a baby, the latter a prim Christian missionary; Iona receives a love letter from her Cherokee sweetheart St Julian Last Child asking her to stay with him in the islands; Eula and Eli's future is clouded by the child they are expecting as a result of Eula's rape, presumably by a white man. The narrative's provision of multiple perspectives follows African narrative traditions rather than the individualism of European story-telling, or, as Bambara puts it: 'Communalism is the major mode of the production' (1993: 124). The perspectives of Nana Peazant and Eula's unborn child are privileged by the voice-over narration they provide, stressing and linking past and future ('the ancestors and the womb are one', in Nana's words).

At the end of the film, a small group remain at Ibo Landing: Nana, Yellow Mary, Eula, Eli and their unborn child, and Iona, who is swept up at the moment of embarcation by St Julian Last Child on a white horse. Disregarding the 1990s fashion for nomadism, Dash romances the notion of home.[9] This is accomplished without recourse to concepts of cultural purity: the islanders encompass ethnic, religious, cultural and sexual differences, and there is continual reference to their island home as a place of transition which holds memories of great suffering. The manner in which the film resolves past and present, cultural identity and cultural hybridity, is best demonstrated by the way it deals with Eula's pregnancy. Nana helps Eli come to terms with it by arguing that, whatever her paternity, the child is sent by the ancestors. Eula chides some of the women for shunning Yellow Mary, telling them that she also is 'ruined', as were all their mothers:

> Even though you're going up North, you all think about being ruined, too. You think you can cross over to the mainland and run away from it? You're going to be sorry, sorry, if you don't change your way of thinking before you leave this place. (Dash et al 1992: 156)

In *Daughters of the Dust*, cultural integrity is not a matter of racial purity, but of shared memory. The dense mise-en-scène of the film is the outcome of years of historical research with the intention of restoring a link in popular memory:

> The film's respectful attention to languages, codes of conduct, food preparation, crafts, chair caning, hair sculptures, quilt making, and mural painting constitutes a praise song to the will and imagination of a diasporized and besieged people to forge a culture that can be sustained. (Bambara 1993: 127)

This aesthetic extends to the filmic as well as the pro-filmic, for instance in the variations in frame rate used by cinematographer A. J. Fiedler to suggest in the co-existence of different temporalities a diasporic relationship between experience and time. *Daughters of the Dust* is a deliberately challenging film for most spectators to watch, as Bambara points out:

> *Daughters of the Dust* demands some work on the part of the spectator whose ear and eye have been conditioned by habits of viewing industry fare that masks history and addicts us to voyeurism, fetishism, mystified notions of social relations and freakish notions of intimate relations. (132–3)

Shirin Neshat: exile

Most of the filmmakers discussed in this chapter share Dash's interest in working with formal patterns other than binarism, as far as is possible, equating this fundamental discursive and linguistic trope with the logics of self and other at work in racism and sexism. But the issue of binarism has at times seemed insoluble for alternative and minor cinemas as oppositionality depends, by definition, on the existence of something to oppose – the margins are defined in relation to the mainstream, the minor to the major, the feminine exists only in relation to the masculine, and so on.

An alternative possibility is adumbrated in the work of New York-based Iranian visual artist Shirin Neshat, whose films and installations embrace binarism for a variety of located reasons. As Naficy points out, binarism is a particular feature of exilic films, whereas multiplicity is a feature of diasporic films (2001: 14). Binarism tropes the tension between the absent homeland and the host country and its effects in the experience of doubled subjectivity which some exiles have described. But binarism is also an essential theme of Neshat's work, which explores the effects of sexual segregation in Iran via the profound visual impact its introduction had on the world of her childhood.

Known first for her photography, Neshat began making films in 1996, and has completed a number of two-screen installations and short films. These works explore the culture and iconography of Iran, from which Neshat was exiled after the revolution of 1979, and equally, the synaesthesic potential of film as a medium characterised by combinatory possibilities. Neshat's work combines the imagistic and sculptural aspects of mise-en-scène with the poetic propensities of time-based structure and the emotional impact of music. Technically, her films are realised at a very high level and achieve great beauty, with cinematography by the renowned Iranian director Ghasem Ebrahimiem, and musical scores by Iranian composer and vocalist Sussan Deyhim (excepting *Passage* (2001), which is scored by Philip Glass).

Neshat's two-screen installations, including *Turbulent* (1998), *Soliloquy* (1999) and *Rapture* (1999) are by their very nature concerned with binarism. Naficy connects this binarism to Neshat's exile status: 'The mere exposure to Shirin Neshat's two-monitor avant-garde video installations ... reproduces the duality, fragmentation and simultaneity of exilic liminality' (2001: 78).[10] This is particularly clear in the case of *Soliloquy*, in which Neshat herself appears as the protagonist (revisiting the terrain of Deren's *Meshes of the Afternoon*), and wanders fully veiled, on one screen, in an ancient town of Middle Eastern appearance (actually Mardin in Turkey), and, on the other, in a North American cityscape (Albany, New York); the two environments are counterpointed as, for instance, when simultaneous shots show Neshat standing at a window overlooking urban American rail tracks and highways, and standing at a barred window overlooking a courtyard in Mardin. Neshat appears to belong in neither place. Although none of the footage is shot in Iran, where it is problematic for Neshat to obtain permission to film, the installation conjures up an imaginary Iran (and an imaginary North America). In a manner characteristic of exilic film, *Soliloquy* is shaped by the loss and longing occasioned by this structuring absence.

The earlier *Turbulent* is equally preoccupied with duality, but deals with the duality of the genders rather than the self, and particularly with the strict segregation of sexes enforced in Iran by the Islamic Republic. *Turbulent* is concerned with performance and taboo, and takes as its starting point the official prohibition which prevents women in Iran from performing music in public. On one screen, a man appears, dressed simply in black trousers and white shirt, before an audience composed entirely of similarly dressed men. Facing away from the audience in the film and towards the camera, he performs a traditional Sufi love song, a setting of a poem by the thirteenth-century Persian mystic Jalal al-Din Rumi. On the other side of the room, absolutely separated but for a false eyeline match between the two screens, a woman dressed in a black chador performs in an empty auditorium. Her wordless song, composed and performed by Deyhim, is a plangent and ecstatic free-form extemporisation; the male singer, on the other screen, appears transfixed by her passionately transgressive performance. While the piece conveys the expected critique of repressive social arrangements, its relationship to the symbolic system which underlies them is complex and ambivalent: neither the primal energy of the woman's performance, nor the latent eroticism and austere poetry of the installation could exist without these symbolic laws.

The short film *Pulse* (2001) plays in similar ways with repression and desire, although its formal realisation is very different. A single ten-minute shot shows a woman in a darkened room listening to music on the radio. A bell tolls, a man sings, the woman caresses the radio. The film is black and white, with very low key lighting, and the camera, mounted on a crane, glides slowly towards and away from the woman, tracking and panning with a sensuousness that matches its subject. The room's small barred window suggests cloistered privacy rather than imprisonment, its ornate wrought ironwork echoed by a wrought iron bedstead. Binarism is manifested in the relationship between sound and image, male and female. The setting suggests an obscure desire, hidden from public scrutiny. The simplicity of the film's form gives a heightened sense of the restrictions of Islamic society, but at the same time discloses a repressed or displaced, aestheticised sensuality.

Whereas *Soliloquy, Turbulent* and *Pulse* are concerned with individual displacements and transgressions, the installation *Rapture* (1999) deals with collective experience. Like *Turbulent, Rapture* presents black and white images on two screens, one showing men, the other, women. The men, a group of over a hundred, are dressed in black trousers and white shirts; the women, of whom there are an equal number, wear black chadors. Each group is placed in a symbolic context: the men undertake a series of actions in an ancient seaside fortress, symbolising culture, while the women progress through a harsh and barren desert landscape, symbolising nature. Seeming to observe the men, the women gather and ululate noisily, before turning their backs and heading for the seashore, where six of them embark in a small boat, while the men wave goodbye from the ramparts. As well as structuring the installation around heightened graphic contrasts, Neshat choreographs the movements of the two groups so as to bring out the sculptural qualities of the massed bodies, seen in long and high-angled shots which emphasize their choric quality. The images seem both ancient and modern, ritualistic and abstracted. The overall effect suggests an ancient fable which has been only partially remembered or understood, containing fragments of readable allegory, such as the ruined castle of male enterprise contrasted with the small female group's courageous embarcation into an unknown future, but at the same time slipping through the net of rational interpretation.

The relationship of Neshat's work to the homeland from which she is exiled is profoundly and precisely ambivalent, in the sense that it is structured by the simultaneous presence of opposing values. Neshat critiques Islamic Iran by showing its symbolic structures, particularly the extreme dichotomisation of the genders, in stark relief, but at the same time, her work derives its systems from these ideological structures. In her most effective – and, arguably, most progressive – works, there is a historical layering effect: the revolutionary Iranian imagery is counterpointed against Persian poetry and ecstatic experimental music, adumbrating the erotic magnetism created and denied by separation (binarism too has an opposite). The result is an alternative Iranian imaginary, brought into existence with the help of the talented Iranian exiles who work with Neshat: a collaborative exilic aesthetic which incorporates the binarism of sexual segregation in order to challenge it with a seductive, syncretic poetry. Neshat's films and installations articulate a politics of dislocation, of deterritorialisation and loss, through starkly dichotomised forms. However, there is a danger that beyond the exilic community from which they emerge and which they address in the first instance, their binary patterning will invite readings in terms of the exoticism or demonisation of the Other. In the era of globalisation, the politics of location – and dislocation – are complicated by the possibility that transnational and transcultural reception may revise or even reverse the meanings of artworks.

AFTERWORD: WOMEN'S CINEMA/TRANSNATIONAL CINEMA

Gilles Deleuze observes that in a minor cinema or literature, 'because the people are missing, the author is in a situation of producing utterances which are already collective, which are like the seeds of the people to come' (1989: 221). Likewise, when feminist theories of women's cinema first appeared in the 1970s, there were so few films by women that the theorists were faced with the necessity of inventing or forecasting a practice. Today, although women's filmmaking is still very much a minority activity, there is now enough work in a wide range of styles and from a variety of cultures for a different kind of writing to come to the fore, writing which is historical and comparative.

A number of histories of women's cinema within national boundaries have been written (for instance, see Attwood 1993; Flitterman-Lewis 1990; Knight 1992) but comparative studies of women's cinema are more unusual, and tend to take the form of regional surveys (see, for example, Shohat 1997). In Film Studies, the idea of comparative or cross-cultural analysis is a relatively recent one (see Willemen 1994: 206–19), although in Women's Studies, transnational critical practice is a more influential concept (see Grewal & Kaplan 1994). In both disciplines, there are strong arguments for the development of methods of critical inquiry which foreground transnational cultural and economic interactions. The economics of the film industry make it a transnational medium: production   funds, talent and box-office receipts follow global flows. In the era of globalisation, gender oppression is also inflected by the global movements of capital. As a politics, feminism is bound to respond to globalisation, or else wither away in decadent and wilful blindness to the new forms taken by women's oppression in the 'new world order'.

Deepa Mehta: transnational cultural politics

The complexities of the transnational production and reception of women's cinema are nowhere more marked than in the case of the Indian-Canadian director Deepa Mehta, and her film trilogy *Fire* (1996), *Earth* (1998) and *Water* (not yet completed). The trilogy looks at the social and historical situation of women in India. *Fire*, the first part, is a melodrama which turns a horrified eye on arranged marriage in the Hindu middle class. The second part, *Earth*, a tragic love story set against partition, is concerned with the terrors of sectarian violence. The final film of the trilogy, *Water*, deals with the plight of widows in India. Its shooting was halted in 2000 by the Hindu Right's opposition to its subject matter.

Fire provoked controversy on its release in India and in other countries with substantial Hindu populations for its depiction of a sexual relationship which develops between two women trapped in loveless arranged marriages to brothers. Violent protesters associated with the Hindu fundamentalist organisation Shiv Sena vandalised cinemas and burned posters for the film. Members of the liberal intelligentsia, feminists and some gay/lesbian activists defended the film, although others criticised its lack of commitment to the depiction of lesbian sexual identity and social subjectivity.

In a study of media responses to the film, Sujata Moorti (2000) argues that the controversy demonstrates the complex and conjunctural relationships between global modernity and local 'tradition'. In the decade of the rise to power of the Hindu fundamentalist party, the Bharatiya Janata Party (BJP), Moorti argues, *Fire* provided the occasion for a variety of interest groups to take up public positions on questions of national identity. In the arguments of the Right, a series of fundamentalist propositions are concatenated: the main charge against the film is that, despite its deployment of generic forms from Hindi cinema and traditional cultural references, it lacks authentic Indian identity. The grounds for this include, variously: the director's expatriate status; the 'Western' sexual relationship entered into by the two characters; the slur on Indian womanhood involved in its depiction; and the religion of one of its stars, Shabana Azmi, a well-known Muslim actor. National identity is thus defined through xenophobia, homophobia, sexism and religious bigotry. Moorti notes, nevertheless, that despite its focus on the figure of the woman, the objections to *Fire* are not concerned with its depiction of women *per se*, but with its cultural authenticity. The film becomes part of a wider public sphere within which femininity figures as a nationalist and fundamentalist cipher: 'The controversy over *Fire* occurred at a historical moment when Indian woman was being reconstituted as a diacritic of Hindu nationalism, a specific religious nationalism'. According to Moorti, anxieties regarding the social transformations brought by globalisation coalesce in the hostile responses to the film:

Local resistance to the global is manifested in a series of practices that invoke religion to regulate women; control over female bodies becomes a crucial strategy for rejecting the global. Issues pertaining to female identity, sexuality and social location are repeatedly reworked in the context of global flows. The female body ... becomes a central site where discourses of power and regulation come to bear. (Moorti 2000)

Moorti argues that the controversy over Mehta's film demonstrates the inadequacy of the paradigm which opposes the homogenising effects of global culture to the authentic cultural resistance of the local. In this instance, the transnational, modernising forces of the global are allied with feminism and liberalism (of a bourgeois variety), and they are vigorously contested in the film's local reception, not by popular resistance to the manipulations of global capital, but by a hegemonic nationalism. Moorti suggests that the antinomies global/local and tradition/modernity are both conjunctural rather than universal categories, with no particular meaning or value prior to their emergence at a specific time and place. She also points out that the defenders of Mehta's work – which, it must be admitted, is flawed by schematism and an elite perspective – join its critics in patterning debates around gender identity and cultural nationalism on these paradigmatic oppositions, in the process diverting attention from more complex political realities: 'Those who supported the movie appropriated the female body to narrate a trajectory of progress and modernization. Impelled by different understandings of the global, both Mehta and the religious right opportunistically used the representation of lesbian sexuality' (Moorti 2000). As Grewal & Kaplan argue:

> Global-local as a monolithic formation may also erase the existence of multiple expressions of 'local' identities and concerns and multiple globalities. In this particular way, global-local binaries dangerously correspond to the colonialism-nationalism model that often leaves out various subaltern groups as well as the interplay of power in various levels of sociopolitical agendas. (1994: 11)

To add to the complex challenge of delineating the meanings and effects of Mehta's work, we might consider Arundhati Roy's view that although 'religious bigotry, misogyny, homophobia, book burning and outright hatred are the ways in which to retrieve a nation's lost dignity', they are sponsored by the *same* government which is responsible for the disposal of that dignity:

> How they have evolved and pretty near perfected an extraordinary pincer action – while one arm is busy selling the nation off in chunks, the other, to divert attention, is orchestrating a baying, howling, deranged chorus of cultural nationalism. It would be fascinating to actually see how the inexorable ruthlessness of one process results in the naked, vulgar, terrorism perpetrated by the other. They're Siamese twins ... They share organs. They have the ability to say two entirely contradictory things simultaneously, to hold all positions at all times. There's no separating them. (Roy 2000)

Mehta captures something of this duality in her portrayal of the family in *Fire* – while one of the two brothers is fanatically religious and practices celibacy, the other has distinctly modern tastes which run to Hong Kong action cinema and a Chinese girlfriend. Their arranged marriages represent a hypocritical genuflection to social convention rather than respect for tradition. Mehta's female leads, however, are scarcely situated in relation to these cultural cross-currents, and the film's idealised conclusion, in which they leave their husbands and begin their new lives as lovers with an assignation in a mosque, lifts them from their social ground entirely.

The example of *Fire*, an imperfect women's film, which rises to some of the challenges of transnationalism but fails to negotiate others, gives some indication of the complexities involved, for filmmakers and critics, in posing feminist questions in a world of unequal transnational exchanges. Globalisation poses new challenges for feminism, arising from the import and export of social and economic inequalities, the uneven distribution of access to new technologies and the reinvention of tradition by religious fundamentalists, nationalists and tribal warlords in their disparate opposi- tions to this new imperialism. Women's cinema is well-placed, literally, to address these transnational processes and the interrelationships between them: as minor cinema, it inhabits cultural and political formations without being entirely naturalised there, and at the same time exceeds them, through its lateral affiliations. Its usefulness resides in precisely these qualities: it exists only in the eyes of its beholders, crossing boundaries between forms, periods and cultures to engender feminist communities.

NOTES

INTRODUCTION

1   Johnston committed suicide in 1987, after several years of mental illness, exacerbated by the economic and cultural climate of London in the 1980s. See Morris 1998.
2   Deleuze also applies this concept to cinema, in *Cinema 2: The Time-Image* (1989), although he applies it to post-colonial films rather than women's films, which he scarcely acknowledges.

CHAPTER ONE

1   The Guerrilla Girls stickers are available at their website: http://www.guerrillagirls.com/posters/hwdstlck.html.
2   The Women Film Pioneers Project is based at Duke University. Its website address is: http://www.duke.edu/web/film/pioneers.html.
3   Ida Lupino worked extensively in television, as have many women directors since, including Martha Coolidge, Claudia Weill, Donna Deitch, Joyce Chopra, Susan Seidelman, Allison Anders and Julie Dash.
4   Basinger's description of the woman's film concurs with Mulvey's view, although rather than valuing its incorporation of fantasy, Mulvey sees ideological critique in its depiction of 'recognisable, real and familiar traps, which for women brings it closer to daydream than fairy story' (Mulvey 1977/8: 56). Beyond the woman's film, the lure of fantasy and the recognition of reality have functioned as magnetic poles in the development of women's cinema and the debates concerning the role of the entertainment film within it.
5   'Women in Pairs', *The Village Voice*, April 28, 1975, 78. Quoted in Mayne 1994: 88.
6   This international cycle began outside the US, with Sally Potter's *Orlando* (1992) and Jane Campion's *The Piano* (1993) and has continued with Marleen Gorris's *Mrs Dalloway* (1997) and Patricia Rozema's *Mansfield Park* (1999). Its antecedents include Armstrong's landmark feminist film *My Brilliant Career* (1979). On debates around the new heritage film, see Vincendeau 2001.
7   B. Ruby Rich (2001) and Modleski (1999) both cite Tompkins in their discussions of the film.

CHAPTER TWO

1   J. Hoberman, 'The Maya Mystique', *The Village Voice*, 23, 20, 15 May 1978, 54, quoted in Rabinovitz 1991: 56. The film's opening credits, which read: 'Hollywood 1943' indicate an intentionally ironic stance towards Hollywood.
2   Dates for Schneeman's films vary in different sources. I have followed Schneemann 1997.
3   B. Ruby Rich reports that Schneemann has claimed that the film is shot from the cat's perspective (Rich 1998: 27–8) and David E. James perceives this as a semiotic dirty joke, 'pussy's point of view' (James 1989: 319).
4   *Ontological Leap* is the title of a photo series made by Export in 1974.
5   Serge Daney writes: 'Militant cinema foundered on the question of the voice-over (the protected voice) [...] from the failure of the voiceover we have seen a whole adventure of the voice develop, an adventure that has been conducted "au feminin"' (Daney 1977).
6   The interpretation of the film's narrative trajectory as a lesbian telos is particularly problematic in view of the emphasis placed on orality, most marked in the protagonist's obsessive consumption of sugar, suggesting regression and maternal fixation as a rationale for lesbianism.

CHAPTER THREE

1   For a critical analysis of Kluge's use of female protagonists and his address to female spectators see Schlupmann 1988.
2   John Ellis and Sheila Johnston quoted in Elsaesser 1989: 203.
3   Sex outside of marriage is illegal in Iran.
4   This scene narrowly escaped censorship for impropriety in Iran. The use of children, to whom taboos on contact do not apply, is a common way of working around censorship in Iranian cinema.
5   In Tehran it is illegal for women to cycle.
6   Modleski (1999) discusses a number of critical responses to the film.
7   A contemporary reading of the film is complicated by Jimmy Little's comeback on the world music circuit with a repertoire that includes covers of Nick Cave songs *and* traditional Aborigine songs: assimilation may not be entirely reversible, but it is apparently re-negotiable.
8   Mellencamp explores Moffatt's ambivalences through the theories of Eisenstein and Deleuze (1995a: 268–70).
9   See R. Braidotti (1994) *Nomadic Subjects: Embodiment and Sexual Difference in Contemporary Feminist Theory*. New York: Columbia University Press.
10 Neshat's installations are exhibited on video for practical reasons, although the footage is generated on film.

BIBLIOGRAPHY

Akomfrah, J. (1989) 'Third Scenario: Theory and the Politics of Location', *Framework* 36, 5–6.

Anderson, B. (1991) *Imagined Communities: Reflections on the Origin and Spread of Nationalism*. London: Verso.

Appadurai, A. (1990) 'Disjuncture and Difference in the Global Cultural Economy', *Public Culture*, 2, 2, Spring, 1–23.

Attwood, L. (1993) *Red Women on the Silver Screen: Soviet Women and Cinema from the Beginning to the End of the Communist Era*. London: Pandora.

Bambara, T. C. (1993) 'Reading the Signs, Empowering the Eye: *Daughters of the Dust* and the Black Independent Cinema Movement', in M. Diawara (ed.) *Black American Cinema*. London and New York: Routledge, 118–44.

Basinger, J. (1994) *A Woman's View: How Hollywood Spoke to Women, 1930–1960*. London: Chatto and Windus.

Berger, J. (1972) *Ways of Seeing*. London: BBC and Penguin.

Bruzzi, S. (1997) *Undressing Cinema: Clothing and Identity in the Movies*. London and New York: Routledge.

Clover, C. J. (1992) *Men, Women and Chainsaws: Gender in the Modern Horror Film*. London: British Film Institute.

Comolli, J.-L. and J. Narboni (1971) 'Cinema/Ideology/Criticism', *Screen* 12/1, 27–35.

Cook, P. (1981) 'The Point of Self-Expression in Avant-Garde Film', in J. Caughie (ed.) *Theories of Authorship: A Reader*. London and New York: Routledge and Kegan Paul, 271–81.

____ (1998) 'No Fixed Address: The Women's Picture from *Outrage* to *Blue Steel*', in M. Smith and S. Neale (eds) *Contemporary Hollywood Cinema*. London and New York: Routledge, 229–46.

Daney, S. and B. Krohn (1977) '*Les Cahiers du cinéma* 1968–1977', *The Thousand Eyes*. New York: Bleecker Street Cinema. Available on-line: http://home.earthlink.net/~steevee/Daney_1977.html (20 September 2001).

Dash, J. et al (1992) *Daughters of the Dust: The Making of An African American Woman's Film*. New York: The New Press.

De Lauretis, T. (1984) *Alice Doesn't: Feminism, Semiotics, Cinema*. London: MacMillan.

____ (1987a) 'Strategies of Coherence: Narrative Cinema, Feminist Poetics and Yvonne Rainer', in T. de Lauretis, *Technologies of Gender: Essays on Theory, Film and Fiction*. Bloomington and Indianapolis: Indiana University Press, 107–26.

_____ (1987b) 'Rethinking Women's Cinema: Aesthetics and Feminist Theory', in T. de Lauretis, *Technologies of Gender: Essays on Theory, Film and Fiction*. Bloomington and Indianapolis: Indiana University Press, 127–48.

_____ (1990) 'Guerrilla in the Midst: Women's Cinema in the 80s', *Screen* 31/1, 6–25.

Deleuze, G. (1989) *Cinema 2: The Time-Image*. London: Athlone Press.

Deleuze, G. and F. Guattari (1986) *Kafka: Toward a Minor Literature*. Trans. D. Polan. Minneapolis and Oxford: University of Minnesota Press.

Deren, M. (1965) 'Notes, Essays, Letters', *Film Culture*, 39, 1–86.

Deren, M., et al. (1963) 'Poetry and the Film: a Symposium', *Film Culture*, 29, 55–63.

Dyson, L. (1995) 'The Return of the Repressed? Whiteness, Femininity and Colonialism in *The Piano*', *Screen*, 36/3, 267–76.

Elsaesser, T. (1975) 'The Pathos of Failure: American Films in the 70s', *Monogram* 6, 13–19.

_____ (1989) *New German Cinema: A History*. Basingstoke and London: MacMillan and British Film Institute.

Fischer, L. (1989) *Shot/Countershot: Film Tradition and Women's Cinema*. Basingstoke and London: MacMillan and British Film Institute.

Flitterman-Lewis, S. (1990) *To Desire Differently: Feminism and the French Cinema*. Urbana and Chicago: University of Illinois Press.

Foster, G. A. (ed.) (1999) *Identity and Memory: The Films of Chantal Akerman*. Trowbridge: Flicks Books.

Gaines, J. (1988) 'White Privilege and Looking Relations: Race and Gender in Feminist Film Theory', *Screen*, 29/4, 12–27.

Geraghty, C. (1986) 'Three Women's Films', in C. Brunsdon (ed.) *Films for Women*. London: British Film Institute, 144–5.

Gledhill, C. (1994) 'Image and Voice', in D. Carson, L. Dittmar and J. R. Welsch (eds) *Multiple Voices in Feminist Film Criticism*. Minneapolis and London: University of Minnesota Press, 109–123.

Goldson, A. (1997) 'Piano recital', *Screen*, 38/3, 275–81.

Gordon, B. (1984) '*Variety*: The Pleasure in Looking', in C. S. Vance (ed.) *Pleasure and Danger: Exploring Female Sexuality*. Boston, London, Melbourne and Henley: Routledge and Kegan Paul, 189–203.

Greenberg, C. (1965) 'Modernist Painting', *Art & Literature*, 4, 193–201.

Grewal, I. and C. Kaplan (1994) 'Introduction: Transnational Feminist Practices and Postmodernity', in I. Grewal and C. Kaplan (eds) *Scattered Hegemonies: Postmodernity and Transnational Feminist Practices*. Minneapolis and London: University of Minnesota Press, 1–33.

Guy, A. (1996) 'Woman's Place in Photoplay Production', Trans. R. and S. Blaché, in A. Slide (ed.) *The Memoirs of Alice Guy Blaché*. Lanham, Md, and London: Scarecrow Press, 139–42.

Hansen, M. (1991) *Babel and Babylon: Spectatorship in American Silent Film*. Cambridge: Harvard University Press.

Harper, G. (1998) *Interventions and Provocations: Conversations on Art, Culture and Resistance*. Albany: State University of New York Press.

Haskell, M. (1973) *From Reverence to Rape: The Treatment of Women in the Movies*. New York: Holt, Rinehart and Winston.

hooks, b. (1992) *Black Looks: Race and Representation*. Boston: South End Press.

Huyssen, A. (1988) *After the Great Divide: Modernism, Mass Culture and Postmodernism*. Basingstoke and London: MacMillan.

Indiana, G. (2000) 'Body Double', in E. Longhauser (ed.) *Valie Export: Ob/De+Con(Struction)*. Philadelphia: The Galleries at Moore. Available on-line: http://www.thegalleriesatmoore.org/publications/valiegi.shtml (20 September 2001).

Islam, N. (1995) '"I Wanted to Shoot People" – Genre, Gender and Action in the Films of

Kathryn Bigelow', in L. Jayamanne (ed.) *Kiss Me Deadly: Feminism and Cinema for the Moment*. Sydney: Power Institute of Fine Arts, 91–125.

James, D. E. (1989) *Allegories of Cinema: American Film in the Sixties*. Princeton: Princeton University Press.

Jameson, F. (1992) *The Geopolitical Aesthetic: Cinema and Space in the World System*. London: British Film Institute.

Jayamanne, L. (1992) 'Love Me Tender, Love Me True, Never Let Me Go...', *Framework* 38/9, 87–94.

Jayamanne, L., L. Thornton and T. T. Minh-ha (1992) '"Which Way to Political Cinema?": A Conversation Piece', in T. T. Minh-ha (ed.) *Framer Framed*. New York and London: Routledge, 243–65.

Johnston, C. (1973a) 'Introduction', in C. Johnston (ed.) *Notes on Women's Cinema*. London: Society for Education in Film and Television, 2–4.

____ (1973b) 'Women's Cinema as Counter-Cinema' in C. Johnston (ed.) *Notes on Women's Cinema*. London: Society for Education in Film and Television, 24–31.

____ (1975) 'Dorothy Arzner: Critical Strategies' in C. Johnston (ed.) *The Work of Dorothy Arzner: Towards a Feminist Cinema*. London: British Film Institute, 1–8.

____ (1980) 'The Subject of Feminist Film Theory/Practice', *Screen*, 21/2, 27–34.

____ (1986) '*Maeve*', in C. Brunsdon (ed.) *Films for Women*. London: British Film Institute, 91–8.

Julien, I. and M. Nash (1998) 'Only Angels Have Wings', in L. Cooke and K. Kelly (eds) *Tracey Moffatt: Free-Falling*. New York: Dia Center for the Arts. 9–20.

Kaplan, E. A. (1983) *Women and Film: Both Sides of the Camera*. New York and London: Methuen.

____ (1997) *Looking for the Other: Feminism, Film, and the Imperial Gaze*. New York and London: Routledge.

Kaplan, C. (1994) 'The Politics of Location as Transnational Feminist Practice', in I. Grewal and C. Kaplan (eds) *Scattered Hegemonies: Postmodernity and Transnational Feminist Practices*. Minneapolis and London: University of Minnesota Press, 137–52.

Knight, J. (1992) *Women and the New German Cinema*. London: Verso.

Kristeva, J. (1981) 'Woman can never be defined', in E. Marks and I. de Courtivron (eds) *New French Feminisms: An Anthology*. Brighton: Harvester Press, 137–41.

Kuhn, A. (1982) *Women's Pictures: Feminism and Cinema*. London: Routledge and Kegan Paul.

____ (ed.) (1995) *Queen of the B's: Ida Lupino Behind the Camera*. Trowbridge: Flicks Books.

Lane, C. (2000) *Feminist Hollywood: From Born in Flames to Point Break*. Detroit: Wayne State University Press.

Lauzen, M. D. (2000) *Status of Women in the Industry: Executive Summary: The Real Story on Reel Women: Behind the Scenes Employment in the Top 250 Films of 1999*. New York: New York Women in Film and Television. Available on-line: http://www.nywift.org/resources/status_lauzen.html (20 September 2001).

Lennon, P. (2001) 'Sins of the Mothers', *The Guardian, G2*, 22 June, 11.

MacDonald, S. (1992) *A Critical Cinema 2*. Berkeley and Los Angeles: University of California Press.

Manenti, V. (n.d.) Text quoted on flyer for *Syntagma*, original source unknown.

Margulies, I. (1996) *Nothing Happens: Chantal Akerman's Hyperrealist Everyday*. Durham and London: Duke University Press.

Mayne, J. (1990) *The Woman at the Keyhole: Feminism and Women's Cinema*. Bloomington and Indianapolis: Indiana University Press.

____ (1994) *Directed by Dorothy Arzner*. Bloomington and Indianapolis: Indiana University Press.

McMahan, A. (1999) 'The Effect of Multiform Narrative on Subjectivity', *Screen* 40/2, 146–57.

Mellencamp, P. (1990) *Indiscretions: Avant-Garde Film, Video, and Feminism*. Bloomington and Indianapolis: Indiana University Press.

_____ (1995a) *A Fine Romance: Five Ages of Film Feminism*. Philadelphia: Temple University Press.

_____ (1995b) 'Five Ages of Film Feminism', in L. Jayamanne (ed.) *Kiss Me Deadly: Feminism and Cinema for the Moment*. Sydney: Power Institute of Fine Arts, 18–76.

Mitchell, J. (2000) *Mad Men and Medusas*. London: Penguin.

Modleski, T. (1999) *Old Wives' Tales: Feminist Re-Visions of Film and Other Fictions*. London and New York: I. B. Tauris.

Moorti, S. (2000) 'Inflamed Passions: *Fire*, the Woman Question, and the Policing of Cultural Borders', *Genders OnLine Journal*, 32. Available on-line: http://www.gendersorg/g32/g32_moorti.html (20 February 2002).

Morris, M. (1988) *The Pirate's Fiancée: Feminism, Reading, Postmodernism*. London: Verso.

_____ (1998) *Too Soon Too Late: History in Popular Culture*. Bloomington and Indianapolis: Indiana University Press.

Mueller, R. (1994) *Valie Export: Fragments of the Imagination*. Bloomington and Indianapolis: Indiana University Press.

Mulvey, L. (1975) 'Visual Pleasure and Narrative Cinema', *Screen*, 16/3, 6–18.

_____ (1977/8) 'Notes on Sirk and Melodrama', *Movie*, 25, 53–6.

_____ (1979) 'Film, Feminism and the Avant-Garde', *Framework*, 10, 3–10.

_____ (1981) 'Afterthoughts on 'Visual Pleasure and Narrative Cinema' inspired by *Duel in the Sun*', *Framework*, 15/16/17, 12–15.

_____ (1986) 'Melodrama in and out of the home', in C. MacCabe (ed.) *High Theory/Low Culture: Analysing Popular Television and Film*. Manchester: Manchester University Press, 80–100.

_____ (1987) 'Changes: Thoughts on Myth, Narrative and Historical Experience', *History Workshop Journal*, 23, 3–19.

_____ (1995) 'Moving Bodies', *Sight and Sound*, 5/3, 18–20.

Naficy, H. (1996) 'Iranian Cinema', in G. Nowell-Smith (ed.) *The Oxford History of World Cinema*. Oxford: Oxfrod University Press, 672–8.

_____ (2000) 'Parallel Worlds' in G. Mackert (ed.) *Shirin Neshat*. Vienna and London: Kunsthalle Wien and Serpentine Gallery, 43–53.

_____ (2001) *An Accented Cinema: Exilic and Diasporic Filmmaking*. New Jersey: Princeton University Press.

Neale, S. (2000) *Genre and Hollywood*. London: Routledge.

Ostrowska, E. (1998) 'Filmic Representations of the "Polish Mother" in Post-Second World War Polish Cinema', *The European Journal of Women's Studies*, 5, 419–35.

Peary, G. (1977) 'Alice Guy Blaché: Czarina of the Silent Screen', in K. Kay (ed.) *Women and the Cinema: A Critical Anthology*. New York: Dutton, 139–145.

Peiss, K. (1986) *Cheap Amusements: Working Women and Leisure in Turn-of-the-Century New York*. Philadelphia: Temple University Press.

Penley, C. and J. Bergstrom (1985) 'The Avant-Garde: Histories and Theories', in B. Nichols (ed.) *Movies and Methods II*. Berkeley, Los Angeles and London: University of California Press.

Pfeil, F. (1994) 'No Basta Teorizar: In-Difference to Solidarity in Contemporary Fiction, Theory, and Practice', in I. Grewal and C. Kaplan (eds) *Scattered Hegemonies: Postmodernity and Transnational Feminist Practices*. Minneapolis and London: University of Minnesota Press, 197–230.

Rabinovitz, L. (1991) *Points of Resistance: Women, Power and Politics in the New York Avant-Garde Cinema, 1943–71*. Urbana and Chicago: University of Illinois Press.

Reynaud, B. (1987) 'Impossible Projections', *Screen*, 28/4, 40–52.

Rich, A. (1986) *Blood, Bread, and Poetry: Selected Prose*. New York: W. W. Norton.

Rich, B. R. et al (1978) 'Women and Film: A Discussion of Feminist Aesthetics', *New German Critique*, 13, 26–30.

Rich, B. R. (1998) *Chick Flicks: Theories and Memories of the Feminist Film Movement*. Durham and London: Duke University Press.

_____ (2001) 'At Home on the Range', in J. Hillier (ed.) *American Independent Cinema: A Sight and Sound Reader*. London: British Film Institute, 233–9.

Roy, A. (2000) 'Power Politics: the Renaissence of Rumpelstiltskin', *Outlook India.com*. Available on-line: http://www.zmag.org/roy.htm (20 February 2002).

Said, E. W. (2000) 'The Art of Displacement: Mona Hatoum's Logic of Irreconcilables', in S. Wagstaff (ed.) *Mona Hatoum: The Entire World as a Foreign Land*. London: Tate Gallery, 7–17.

Schlupmann, H. (1988) '"What is Different is Good": Women and Femininity in the Films of Alexander Kluge', *October*, 46, 129–50.

Schneemann, C. (1997) *More Than Meat Joy: Performance Works & Selected Writings*. B. R. McPherson (ed.) 2nd edition. Kingston, NY: McPherson.

Shohat, E. (1997) 'Framing Post-Third-Worldist Culture: Gender and Nation in Middle Eastern/ North African Film and Video', *Jouvert* 1/1. Available on-line: http://social.chass.ncsu.edu/ jouvert/v1i1/shohat.htm (20 September 2001).

Sieglohr, U. (1998) 'New German Cinema', in J. Hill and P. Church Gibson (eds) *Oxford Guide to Film Studies*. Oxford: Oxford University Press, 466–70.

Silverman, K. (1988) *The Acoustic Mirror: The Female Voice in Psychoanalysis and Cinema*. Bloomington and Indianapolis: Indiana University Press.

Sitney, P. A. (1979) *Visionary Film: The American Avant-Garde, 1943–78*. 2nd edition. New York: Oxford University Press.

Slide, A. (1996) *The Silent Feminists: America's First Women Directors*. Lanham, Md, and London: Scarecrow Press.

Smelik, A. (1998) *And the Mirror Cracked: Feminist Cinema and Film Theory*. Basingstoke and New York: Palgrave.

Smith, M. (1998) 'Theses on the Philosophy of Hollywood History', in M. Smith and S. Neale (eds) *Contemporary Hollywood Cinema*. London and New York: Routledge, 3–20.

Spinelli, C. (1997) 'Interview', in M. Archer, G. Brett and C. de Zegher (eds) *Mona Hatoum*. London: Phaidon, 134–41.

Stacey, J. (1987) 'Desperately Seeking Difference', *Screen*, 28/1, 48–61.

Stam, R., R. Burgoyne and S. Flitterman-Lewis (1992) *New Vocabularies in Film Semiotics: Structuralism, Post-Structuralism and Beyond*. London and New York: Routledge.

Suter, J. (1988) 'Feminine Discourse in Christopher Strong', in C. Penley (ed.) *Feminism and Film Theory*. London and New York: British Film Institute and Routledge, 89–103.

Tasker, Y. (1993) *Spectacular Bodies: Gender, Genre and the Action Movie*. London and New York: Routledge.

Tompkins, J. (1992) *West of Everything: The Inner Life of Westerns*. New York and Oxford: Oxford University Press.

Trinh, M.-h. T. (1989) 'Outside In Inside Out ', in J. Pines and P. Willemen (eds) *Questions of Third Cinema*. London: British Film Institute, 133–49.

Tscherkassky, P. (1994) 'Mara Mattuschka', in M. Arnold and P. Tscherkassky (eds) *Austrian Avant-Garde Cinema 1955–1993*. San Francisco: Sixpack Film (no page numbers).

Turim, M. (1999) 'Personal pronouncements in *I ... You ... He ... She* and *Portrait of a Young Girl at the end of the 1960s in Brussels*', in G. A. Foster (ed.) *Identity and Memory: The Films of Chantal Akerman*. Trowbridge: Flicks Books, 9–26.

Vincendeau, G. (ed.) (2001) *Film/Literature/Heritage: A Sight and Sound Reader*. London: British Film Institute.

White, P. (1999) *Uninvited: Classical Hollywood Cinema and Lesbian Representability*. Bloomington and Indianapolis: Indiana University Press.

Willemen, P. (1994) *Looks and Frictions: Essays in Cultural Studies and Film Theory*. London: British Film Institute.

Woolf , V. (1967) *Orlando*. Harmondsworth: Penguin.

_____ (1996) 'The Cinema', in M. O'Pray (ed.) *The British Avant-Garde Film, 1926–1995: An Anthology of Writings*. London and Luton: The Arts Council of England/John Libbey Media/ University of Luton, 33–6.

Youngblood, D. (1970) *Expanded Cinema*. London: Studio Vista.

INDEX OF NAMES